Contents

Acknowledgements

Sinéad de Valera, "The Captive Princess" from *The Emerald Ring and Other Irish Fairy Tales* is reprinted by permission of J. C. Fallon Ltd., Dublin.

Walter de la Mare, "The Riddle" from *The Collected Tales of Walter de la Mare* is reprinted by permission of The Society of Authors, London, as representative of the literary trustees of Walter de la Mare.

Ray Bradbury, "A Piece of Wood" from *Long After Midnight* (1978) is reprinted by permission of Intercontinental Literary Agency, London.

Liam O'Flaherty, "His First Flight" from *The Short Stories of Liam O'Flaherty* (1937) is reprinted by permission of Jonathan Cape Ltd., London.

Shirley Jackson, "Charles" from *The Lottery* is reprinted by permission of Farrar, Straus and Giroux, Inc., New York. © 1948 by Shirley Jackson, renewed 1976 by Laurence Hyman, Barry Hyman, Mrs Sarah Webster and Mrs Joanne Schnurer.

James Thurber, "The Princess and the Tin Box" from *The Beast in Me and other Animals* (Harcourt Brace Jovanovich, 1948) is reprinted by permission of Mrs James Thurber. © 1948 by James Thurber, © 1975 by Helen Thurber and Rosemary Thurber Sauers.

Lord Dunsany, "The Speech" from *The Little Tales of Smethers* (1952) is reprinted by permission of Curtis Brown, Ltd., London, on behalf of John Child-Villiers and Valentine Lamb as literary executors of Lord Dunsany.

Robert Turner, "Christmas Gift" is reprinted by permission of the Scott Meredith Literary Agency, Inc., New York. © 1956 by H. S. D. Publications.

Angelica Gibbs, "The Test" is reprinted by permission of The New Yorker Magazine, Inc. © 1940, 1968 by The New Yorker Magazine, Inc.

Dal Stivens, "The Pepper Tree" from *The Scholarly Mouse and Other Tales* (1957) is reprinted by permission of Curtis Brown Ltd., London and Sydney, on behalf of the author. © Dal Stivens.

William Saroyan, "The Great Leapfrog Contest" from *Best Stories of William Saroyan* is reprinted by permission of Laurence Pollinger Ltd., London and the Estate of the late William Saroyan.

Katherine Mansfield, "Her First Ball" is taken from *The Garden Party and Other Stories* (1922).

Twelve Short Masterpieces

Stories and Tales by

Sinéad de Valera · Walter de la Mare
Ray Bradbury · Liam O'Flaherty
Shirley Jackson · James Thurber
Lord Dunsany · Robert Turner
Angelica Gibbs · Dal Stivens
William Saroyan · Katherine Mansfield

Edited by Klaus Burghardt and
Rolf Eisenberg

Ernst Klett Verlag

The cassette accompanying this book contains the stories by Sinéad de Valera, Liam O'Flaherty, Shirley Jackson, James Thurber, Lord Dunsany and Dal Stivens (Klettnummer 57737).

ISBN 3-12-577300-8

1. Auflage 1 [10] | 1991

Alle Drucke dieser Auflage können im Unterricht nebeneinander benutzt werden, sie sind untereinander unverändert. Die letzte Zahl bezeichnet das Jahr dieses Druckes.

Umschlaggestaltung: Hans Lämmle, Stuttgart.
Druck: Gutmann + Co, Heilbronn, Printed in Germany.

Introduction

This collection of stories and tales is intended mainly for young students who are just beginning to read English literature in the original version. For this reason, it has been restricted to really *short* stories, which can as a rule be read and understood at one sitting. This should ensure that little will get in the way of the reader's enjoyment of the stories.

Since the average length of the stories is so short, we have been able to include many different types of story – fairy tale, science fiction, crime, humour, etc. – told from a variety of angles and in widely differing styles. Thus this collection can function as an introductory course on *the art of storytelling*. For example, the reader will become aware of the various points of view from which a story can be told, can study how the various authors create atmosphere and suspense, and learn something about the relationship between fantasy and reality.

The majority of these stories centre around young people (children and young adults), either as main characters, or narrators, or both. For two reasons, it was relatively easy to find such stories for our collection. On the one hand, stories have always been told *to* children, to develop their imagination or to influence their behaviour (cf. our fairy tale). On the other hand, the problems associated with growing up and confronting the adult world have become favourite themes of modern short story writers.

In any case, the stories in our collection will provide plenty of opportunities for identification, whether with a legendary prince and princess, or with a young soldier in an imaginary future; with a teenage girl at her first dance, or even a seagull learning to fly. In addition, the messages hidden in these stories should provide plenty of material for discussion.

Sinéad de Valera

The Captive Princess

Years and years and years ago, when Fionn MacCool in Eirinn and Fionn Gall, a brother giant in Scotland, were building the Giant's Causeway, which was to run between the two countries, there lived in a glen in Antrim a young man named Hugh.

Everyone liked Hugh. He was very kind and neighbourly and it made him sad to see anyone in pain or trouble. He had also a great love for animals.

All the people in the place where Hugh lived had heard of an unhappy princess who had been carried off by a wicked giant and was kept a captive in his castle. This castle was a *crannog* or lake dwelling. It was built on stakes of wood driven down deep in the earth in the centre of the lake. The giant's wife was a witch and if anyone attempted to cross the lake, she set the water in motion and caused it to form whirlpools so that neither swimmer nor boat could reach the castle.

Hugh had a great desire to rescue the princess, whose name was Maca. One day he was sitting in his little house when he heard a wailing sound outside. He went to the door and saw a dog limping by, whining pitifully. He brought the dog into his house and saw that there was a large thorn in one of his front paws. He extracted the thorn and bathed the paw. The dog tried to thank him by licking his hand and then seemed to show that he wished Hugh to follow him. He led him some distance from his house and then turned down a narrow lane with high hedges on each side. At the end of the lane was a tiny little house. An old woman was sitting at the door. She looked very sad but when she saw the dog her face brightened. She thought he had been lost, he was so long away from her. The dog ran forward and put his head in her lap.

"I found this dog outside my house," said Hugh. "There was a thorn in his paw and when I took it out, he seemed to wish me to follow him."

"Good man," said the old woman, "and good dog. He wants me to befriend you as you have befriended him."

Now this old woman was a *bean feasa* (a woman of knowledge), that is, a woman with magic powers and with knowledge of things distant and hidden. She talked with Hugh for some time and he told her of his desire to rescue the princess.

"It is a hard task," said the old woman, "and there are many dangers in the way, but you are strong and brave and you will succeed if you follow my directions."

She went into the house and came out again with a large shell in her hand. Stretched across the shell were silver cords, something like the strings of a lute or violin. The old woman touched the strings and Hugh thought the music was the sweetest he had ever heard.

"Take this shell," said the old woman. "You will come to the Valley of Weasels. They will rush to swarm around you and attack you, but touch the strings lightly and they will become harmless. You will then come to a dark, dense wood through which it will be impossible to pass. Again, touch the strings and all will be well. Next, you must cross a deep, rugged quarry, but at the sound of the music your way will be clear. You have a long journey before you and you will need food."

Again she went into the house. She returned carrying a large oat cake.

"Take this," she said, "and my blessing with it."

"I shall never forget your kindness," said Hugh, as he set off with a stout heart.

It was not long before he reached the valley of weasels. They rushed towards him as if they would spring at this throat. Hugh drew his fingers across the strings of the shell. Immediately the weasels formed a line on each side of him and as he continued to play, they marched along with him till he passed out of the valley.

Next he came to the wood. The trees were so high and so close together that it was impossible for him to pass through. Hugh sounded the strings and all at once the branches parted and the trees themselves seemed to follow him till he came to the far end of the wood.

At last he reached the quarry. There were great jagged rocks on each side and a hollow in the middle. When he began to play, the stones from the bottom rose up and formed a smooth path for him and those at the sides moved gently with him till he reached the farther end.

He now sat down to rest near a clump of sloe bushes. As he was eating his oat cake, a tiny little bird fell from a robin's nest in the bush. He rose at once and gently placed the fledgling back in the nest.

Suddenly a little man stood before him. He had bright, twinkling eyes and a very friendly smile. He handed Hugh a feather, saying as he did so:

'For this your kindly deed
As on your way you speed,
Take this and in your need
Twill serve you well.

By the side of the water which surrounds the giant's castle you will see a seagull. Strike the bird with this feather.

Now haste away,
Make no delay,
Ere close of day,
All will be well."

Having said this, the little man vanished.

Hugh continued his journey. After a time he again sat down to rest and eat some more of the cake. Just above him was an old oak tree with ivy climbing along the trunk. A bat had in some strange way got entangled in the ivy and could not move and there it remained, with the glaring sunshine hurting its poor eyes. Hugh climbed up the tree and placed the bat on the shady side, hidden by the ivy and protected by the branches of the oak.

Again he heard the words:

"For this your kindly deed,
As on your way you speed,
Take this and in your need,
'Twill serve you well."

There stood the little man, handing Hugh a bat's wing. "If you turn this around three times in your right hand, darkness thick as night will fall about you. This darkness will last for a short time only.

Now haste away,
Make no delay,
Ere close of day,
All will be well."

Like a flash the little man was gone.

When Hugh had travelled for some time, he sat down on a stone by the roadside. From the other side of the hedge came a sound as if some creature were in pain. He went through the hedge to the place from which the sound came. There he saw a cat down in a deep well and unable to climb out. Hugh took off his coat and, leaning over the edge of the well, lowered it towards the cat. Puss caught it with her forepaws and Hugh dragged her to safety.

"For this your kindly deed,
As on your way you speed,
Take this and in your need,
'Twill serve you well."

There stood the little man, handing Hugh a cat's eye. "Take this," he said, "and if you hold it in front of you, the darkest way will become bright and clear before you.

Now haste away,
Make no delay,
Ere close of day,
All will be well."

Again the little man disappeared.

Hugh journeyed on. After a time he came in sight of a huge stone castle built in the centre of a lake. This he knew to be the giant's home. At one of the top windows he caught sight of a beautiful, sad face and he knew that the Princess Maca was a captive there.

As Hugh came near the castle he saw the giant and his wife standing on the steps. When the pair saw Hugh, the giant waved his club round his head and the woman raised her wand over the water. Immediately it foamed and turned in all directions and formed whirlpools all round the castle.

Hugh felt it would be impossible to cross that dangerous lake but just then he saw perched on the bank beside him a beautiful seagull. Remembering the little man's advice, he struck the seagull with the feather. All at once the bird became so large and strong that Hugh mounted on its back and was carried across to the castle. When he descended from the back of the bird it flew up into the air.

The giant and his wife rushed down the steps but Hugh waved the bat's wing and in the darkness the pair lost their footing and fell headlong into the water. The whirlpools dragged them down, down and they were never heard of again.

By the light of the cat's eye, Hugh ascended the stairs to the room where the Princess Maca was. As he reached the door, the darkness disappeared and Hugh turned the key which was on the outside of the lock.

Maca told him she was the daughter of the King of Ulster.

"My father," said she, "banished from his kingdom a wicked giant. The giant's brother in revenge seized me and kept me imprisoned here."

"But," said Hugh, "how did the giant take you from your father's home? Are there not guards and attendants there?"

"Yes," said Maca, "but the giant found out that I liked to walk alone in a lovely wood which is near the palace. One spring day as I was gathering violets, he came and bore me away so quickly that I could not even call for help."

"Where is your father's castle?" Hugh asked.

"It is near the western coast and is so far away that I fear I shall never see my home again."

Hugh led the princess down to the water's edge. There stood the seagull. Hugh touched it with the feather. As he did it grew so large that he and

Maca were able to mount on its back. It flew westwards over lakes and plains, over hills and valleys, till it reached a beautiful glen in the midst of the blue hills of Donegal.

There stood the castle before them, its windows shining like gold in the rays of the setting sun.

They dismounted from the seagull and the bird flew swiftly away.

No words can describe the joy of the king and queen when they saw their daughter again. Maca told her parents all about her escape from the giant's castle and of Hugh's kindness and courage.

"You are a brave man," said the king, "and I should like to make you one of the chieftains of the kingdom."

"That would be a great honour," said Hugh, "and nothing would please me better except something which is almost too good to ask for."

"I know what that is," said the queen. "It is our daughter's hand in marriage."

Hugh looked at Maca.

She placed her hand in his, saying, "As I have already given you my heart, you may now take my hand."

The happy pair were married amid scenes of great rejoicing and lived happily ever after.

Biographical Notes

Sinéad Ó Flannagáin was born in a seaside town near Dublin in 1879. While studying to be a teacher, she met and married Eamon de Valera, who was a lecturer in mathematics at the time; he was one of the leaders of the fight for Irish independence, 1916–21, and later became President of the Republic.

Mrs de Valera showed a great patriotic interest in the survival of the Gaelic language. She was the author of several stories for children in Gaelic and also translated a number of children's books into this language.

In the fifties and sixties she published several collections of traditional stories in English: The Emerald Ring and Other Irish Fairy Tales, The Magic Girdle and Other Stories, *and* Fairy Tales of Ireland.

She died at the age of 96 in Dublin and is survived by five sons, two daughters, and numerous grandchildren.

Annotations

6 **Sinéad** [ʃɪ'ne:d] Gaelic form of 'Jane' or 'Janet' – **de Valera** [devə'leərə] – 1 **Fionn MacCool** ['fɪn mə'ku:l] – **Eirinn** ['e:rɪn] *Gael.* Ireland (dative case of 'Eire') – **Fionn Gall** ['fɪn'gɔ:l] *Gael.* (anglicized form: 'Fingal', as in 'Fingal's Cave') – 2 **giant** ['dʒaɪənt] (in fairy tales) person or creature of unusually great size – **causeway** ['kɔ:zweɪ] raised road across low ground or shallow water – **Giant's Causeway** a rock formation of crystallized lava on the north coast of Ireland (near Portrush) – 3 **glen** narrow valley (from *Gael.* 'gleann') – **Antrim** county in the North of Ireland – 4 **Hugh** [hju:] – 8 **wicked** ['wɪkɪd] morally bad – **captive** ['kæptɪv] prisoner – 9 **crannog** [krɑ'no:g/'krænəg] *Gael.* – **dwelling** house, residence – 10 **stake** pole – 11 **witch** Hexe – **to set in motion** to start moving – 12 **whirlpool** ['wɜ:lpu:l] water moving rapidly in a circle – 14 **Maca** ['mɔkə] – 15 **to wail** to utter a long cry of pain or suffering – 16 **to limp** to walk unevenly because of a hurt or stiff leg – **to whine** to make a high, sad sound – 18 **paw** foot of an animal (with claws) – **to extract** to pull out – 21 **lane** narrow road, path – 25 **lap** Schoß – 30 **bean feasa** ['ban'fasə] *Gael.*

7 4 **shell** hard covering of a small sea animal – 6 **lute** [lu:t] stringed musical instrument (Laute) – 9 **weasel** small thin animal with a thick fur – 11 **dense** [dens] thick – 12 **rugged** ['rʌgɪd] *here:* wild and rocky – **quarry** [ɒ] large man-made hole from which stone is obtained (Steinbruch) – 15 **oat cake** cake or bread made of oats (Hafer) – 17 **stout** *here:* brave – 26 **to part** to spread apart, leaving a space in the middle – 28 **jagged** ['dʒægɪd] rough and with sharp edges – 29 **hollow** ['hɒləʊ] *(n.)* hole, piece of lower ground – 30 **smooth** [ð] flat, not rough – 32 **sloe** [sləʊ] Schlehe – 33 **robin** songbird with a red breast – 34 **fledgling** young bird – 37 **deed** a thing done – 40 **'twill** = it will

8 2 **seagull** common white seabird – 3 **to haste** [heɪst] to hurry – 5 **ere** *poet.* before – 7 **to vanish** to disappear – 9 **oak** Eiche – **ivy** ['aɪvɪ] evergreen climbing plant (Efeu) – 10 **trunk** the main stem of a tree – **bat** small, mouselike flying animal (Fledermaus) – **to get entangled** to get caught (in) – 11 **to glare** to shine unpleasantly bright – 28 **creature** ['kri:tʃə] – 30 **well** hole drilled into the earth for obtaining water – 32 **Puss** child's name for a cat

9 11 **club** heavy stick with one thick end – 12 **wand** [ɒ] stick with magic powers (Zauberstab) – **to foam** to form bubbles – 15 **to perch** (of a bird) to sit or rest on s.th. – **bank** land beside a lake or river – 17 **to mount** to get up on – 18 **to descend** [dɪ'send] to come down – 21 **to lose one's footing** to stumble, to lose one's balance – **headlong** head first, falling without control – 24 **to ascend** [ə'send] to climb, to go up – 27 **Ulster** northern province of Ireland – 28 **to banish** to send out of the country as a punishment – 29 **to seize** [si:z] to catch, to carry away by force – 31 **attendant** servant – 34 **to bear (bore, borne)** to carry – **violet** ['vaɪələt] small dark-blue flower (Veilchen)

10 3 **Donegal** ['dʌnɪgɔ:l] county in the north-west of Ireland – 5 **ray** narrow beam of light – **to set** (of the sun) to sink below the horizon – 6 **swift** quick – 11 **chieftain** ['tʃi:ftən] leader of a tribe or clan – 19 **amid** among, surrounded by – **rejoicing** activities expressing happiness and joy

Walter de la Mare

The Riddle

So these seven children, Ann, and Matilda, James, William and Henry, Harriet and Dorothea, came to live with their grandmother. The house in which their grandmother had lived since her childhood was built in the time of the Georges. It was not a pretty house, but roomy, substantial, and square; and an elm tree outstretched its branches almost to the windows.

When the children were come out of the cab (five sitting inside and two beside the driver), they were shown into their grandmother's presence. They stood in a little black group before the old lady, seated in her bow window. And she asked them each their names, and repeated each name in her kind, quavering voice. Then to one she gave a work-box, to William a jack-knife, to Dorothea a painted ball; to each a present according to age. And she kissed all her grandchildren to the youngest.

"My dears," she said, "I wish to see all of you bright and gay in my house. I am an old woman, so that I cannot romp with you; but Ann must look to you, and Mrs Fenn too. And every morning and every evening you must all come in to see your granny; and bring me smiling faces, that call back to my mind my own son Harry. But all the rest of the day, when school is done, you shall do just as you please, my dears. And there is only one thing, just one, I would have you remember. In the large spare bedroom that looks out on the slate roof there stands in the corner an old oak chest; ay, children, older than I, my dears, a great deal older; older than my grandmother. Play anywhere else in the house, but not there." She spoke kindly to them all, smiling at them; but she was very aged, and her eyes seemed to see nothing of this world.

And the seven children, though at first they were gloomy and strange, soon began to be happy and at home in the great house. There was much to interest and to amuse them there; all was new to them. Twice every day, morning and evening, they came in to see their grandmother, who every day seemed more feeble; and she spoke pleasantly to them of her mother, and her childhood, but never forgetting to visit her store of sugar-plums. And so the weeks passed by.

It was evening twilight when Henry went upstairs from the nursery by himself to look at the oak chest. He pressed his fingers into the carved fruit and flowers, and spoke to the dark smiling heads at the corners; and then, with a glance over his shoulder, he opened the lid and looked in. But the chest concealed no treasure, neither gold nor baubles, nor was there anything to alarm the eye. The chest was empty, except that it was lined with silk of old rose, seeming darker in the dusk, and smelling sweet of potpourri. And while Henry was looking in, he heard the softened laughter and the clinking of the cups downstairs in the nursery; and out at the window he saw the day darkening. These things brought strangely to his memory his mother, who in her glimmering white dress used to read to him in the dusk; and he climbed into the chest; and the lid closed gently down over him.

When the other six children were tired with their playing, they filed into their grandmother's room as usual for her goodnight and her sugar-plums. She looked out between the candles at them as if she were unsure of something in her thoughts. The next day Ann told her grandmother that Henry was not anywhere to be found.

"Dearie me, child. Then he must be gone away for a time," said the old lady. She paused. "But remember all of you, do not meddle with the oak chest."

But Matilda could not forget her brother Henry, finding no pleasure in playing without him. So she would loiter in the house thinking where he might be. And she carried her wood doll in her bare arms, singing under her breath all she could make up about him. And when in a bright morning she peeped in on the chest, so sweet-scented and secret it seemed that she took her doll with her into it – just as Henry himself had done.

So Ann, and James, and William, Harriet and Dorothea were left at home to play together. "Some day maybe they will come back to you, my dears," said their grandmother, "or maybe you will go to them. Heed my warning as best you may."

Now Harriet and William were friends together, pretending to be sweethearts; while James and Dorothea liked wild games of hunting, and fishing, and battles.

On a silent afternoon in October Harriet and William were talking softly together, looking out over the slate roof at the green fields, and they heard the squeak and frisking of a mouse behind them in the room. They went together and searched for the small, dark hole from whence it had come out. But finding no hole, they began to finger the carving of the chest, and to give names to the dark-smiling heads, just as Henry had done. "I know! Let's pretend you are Sleeping Beauty, Harriet," said William, "and I'll be the Prince that squeezes through the thorns and comes in." Harriet looked gently and strangely at her brother; but she got into the box and lay down, pretending to be fast asleep; and on tiptoe William leaned over, and seeing how big was the chest he stepped in to kiss the Sleeping Beauty and to wake her from her quiet sleep. Slowly the carved lid turned on its noiseless hinges. And only the clatter of James and Dorothea came in sometimes to recall Ann from her book.

But their old grandmother was very feeble, and her sight dim, and her hearing extremely difficult.

Snow was falling through the still air upon the roof; and Dorothea was a fish in the oak chest, and James stood over the hole in the ice, brandishing a walking-stick for a harpoon, pretending to be an Esquimau. Dorothea's face was red, and her wild eyes sparkled through her tousled hair. And James had a crooked scratch upon his cheek. "You must struggle, Dorothea, and then I shall swim back and drag you out. Be quick now!" He shouted with laughter as he was drawn into the open chest. And the lid closed softly and gently down as before.

Ann, left to her self, was too old to care overmuch for sugar-plums, but she would go solitary to bid her grandmother goodnight; and the old lady looked wistfully at her over her spectacles. "Well, my dear," she said with trembling head; and she squeezed Ann's fingers between her own knuckled finger and thumb. "What lonely old people we are, to be sure!" Ann kissed her grandmother's soft, loose cheek. She left the old lady sitting in her easy chair, her hands upon her knees, and her head turned sidelong towards her.

When Ann was gone to bed she used to sit reading her book by candle-light. She drew up her knees under the sheets, resting her book upon them. Her story was about fairies and gnomes; and the gently-flowing moonlight of the narrative seemed to illumine the white pages, and she could hear in fancy fairy voices, so silent was the great many-roomed house, and so mellifluent were the words of the story. Presently she put out her candle, and, with a confused babel of voices close to her ears, and faint swift pictures before her eyes, she fell asleep.

And in the dead of night she arose out of bed in dream, and with eyes wide open yet seeing nothing of reality, moved silently through the vacant house. Past the room where her grandmother was snoring in brief, heavy slumber, she stepped light and surely, and down the wide staircase. And Vega the far-shining stood over against the window above the slate roof. Ann walked in the strange room as if she were being guided by the hand toward the oak chest. There, just as if she was dreaming it was her bed, she laid herself down in the old rose silk, in the fragrant place. But it was so dark in the room that the movement of the lid was indistinguishable.

Through the long day, the grandmother sat in her bow window. Her lips were pursed, and she looked with dim, inquisitive scrutiny upon the street where people passed to and fro, and vehicles rolled by. At evening she climbed the stair and stood in the doorway of the large spare bedroom. The ascent had shortened her breath. Her magnifying spectacles rested upon her nose. Leaning her hand on the doorpost she peered in towards the glimmering square of window in the quiet gloom. But she could not see far, because her sight was dim and the light of day feeble. Nor could she detect the faint fragrance, as of autumnal leaves. But in her mind was a tangled skein of memories – laughter and tears, and little children now old-fashioned, and the advent of friends, and long farewells. And gossiping fitfully, inarticulately, with herself, the old lady went down again to her window-seat.

Biographical Notes

Walter de la Mare, English poet, novelist, essayist and critic, was born in Kent in 1873 of a Scottish Huguenot family. He attended St. Paul's Cathedral Choir School, London, where he founded and edited a school-magazine.

After leaving school he worked for eighteen years as a clerk in the London offices of the Anglo-American Standard Oil Company. During these years he published some short stories, a volume of verse and a novel. When he was granted a small pension from the British Government in 1908, he was able to direct all his attention to writing.

His talent as a poet was widely recognized after the publication of The Listeners and Other Poems *in 1912. He became really well known when his novel* Memoirs of a Midget *(1921) won the Tait Black Memorial Prize for 1922. Besides that he was awarded a number of other literary prizes for his novels and poems.*

In his later life he received several honorary university degrees and public honours. He died in 1956.

Walter de la Mare is widely known as a poet of gentle fantasy and is regarded by many as the supreme poet of childhood. There is no doubt about his great skill in creating atmosphere. His poems are full of half-heard whispers, moonlight, and mystery. His novels and short stories again and again deal with the supernatural and the macabre.

Annotations

13 4 **the Georges** the Kings from George I to George IV (1714–1830) – 5 **elm tree** large, tall tree with broad leaves (Ulme) – 6 **cab** *here:* horse-drawn carriage (modern meaning: taxi) – 8 **bow window** curved window forming an alcove – 10 **to quaver** to tremble from weakness – **work-box** container for small things needed for sewing, such as needles and thread – 11 **jack-knife** small folding knife – 14 **to romp** to play noisily with a lot of running and jumping – 20 **slate** flat, thin grey stone (Schiefer) – **oak** large tree with hard wood (Eiche) – **chest** large wooden box – 25 **gloomy** sad, depressed – 29 **feeble** weak, as from old age – 30 **store** collection of things put aside for later use – 32 **nursery** room in which children can play – 33 **to carve** to form by cutting away the surrounding wood or stone

14 3 **to conceal** [–'–] to hide – **bauble** cheap jewel – 4 **to line s.th.** to cover the inside of s.th. (with cloth) – 5 **dusk** time just before it gets quite dark – **pot-pourri** [ˌpəʊ'pʊəri] mixture of dried pieces of sweet-smelling flowers and leaves kept in a jar – 9 **glimmering** shining – 11 **to file** to walk one after the other – 17 **do not meddle with** stay away from – 20 **to loiter** to stand or move about aimlessly – 23 **to peep** to look at s.th. quickly and secretly – **sweet-scented** smelling sweet – 27 **to heed** to pay attention to – 34 **to frisk** to run and jump about playfully – 38 **Sleeping Beauty** Dornröschen – 39 **to squeeze** (through) to force oneself through

15 4 **hinge** [hɪndʒ] metal part on which a lid or door turns or swings – 6 **dim (sight)** bad eyesight – 9 **to brandish** to wave around in the air; to swing – 10 **Esquimau** ['eskɪməʊ] also spelt 'Eskimo' – 11 **to sparkle** to send out little flashes of light – **tousled** [aʊ] untidy; in disorder – 12 **crooked** ['krʊkɪd] not straight – 17 **solitary** quite alone; without friends – 18 **wistful** melancholy – 19 **knuckled** *here:* bent at the knuckles (Knöchel) – 21 **easy chair** armchair – 25 **fairy, gnome** [nəʊm] small, imaginary beings – 28 **mellifluent** [me'lɪflʊənt] *usu.* **mellifluous** sweet-sounding – 29 **babel** ['beɪbəl] mixture of voices which are impossible to understand – 32 **vacant** ['veɪkənt] empty – 35 **Vega** name of a star – 38 **fragrant** ['freɪgrənt] sweet-smelling; *noun:* **fragrance** – 39 **indistinguishable** impossible to see (a difference, a movement etc.)

16 2 **to purse (lips)** to press one's lips together – **inquisitive** [ɪŋ'kwɪzɪtɪv] curious, wanting to know s.th. – **scrutiny** ['skru:tɪnɪ] close and very careful look – 5 **ascent** climb, upward movement – **(magnifying) spectacles** glasses – 6 **to peer** to look closely at s.th. that is difficult to see – 7 **gloom** darkness – 9 **tangled skein** [skeɪn] confused mass (of threads) – 11 **advent** ['––] arrival – **to gossip** *here:* to talk a lot about unimportant things (usually about other people) – **fitfully** restlessly – **inarticulately** [ˌɪnɑ:'tɪkjʊlətlɪ] not speaking clearly

Ray Bradbury

A Piece of Wood

"Sit down, young man," said the Official.

"Thanks." The young man sat.

"I've been hearing rumors about you," the Official said pleasantly. "Oh, nothing much. Your nervousness. Your not getting on so well. Several months now I've heard about you, and I thought I'd call you in. Thought maybe you'd like your job changed. Like to go overseas, work in some other War Area? Desk job killing you off, like to get right in on the old fight?"

"I don't think so," said the young sergeant.

"What *do* you want?"

The sergeant shrugged and looked at his hands. "To live in peace. To learn that during the night, somehow, the guns of the world had rusted, the bacteria had turned sterile in their bomb casings, the tanks had sunk like prehistoric monsters into roads suddenly made tar pits. That's what I'd like."

"That's what we'd all like, of course," said the Official. "Now stop all that idealistic chatter and tell me where you'd like to be sent. You have your choice – the Western or the Northern War Zone." The Official tapped a pink map on his desk.

But the sergeant was talking at his hands, turning them over, looking at the fingers: "What would you officers do, what would we men do, what would the *world* do if we all woke tomorrow with the guns in flaking ruin?"

The Official saw that he would have to deal carefully with the sergeant. He smiled quietly. "That's an interesting question. I like to talk about such theories, and my answer is that there'd be mass panic. Each nation would think itself the only unarmed nation in the world, and would blame its enemies for the disaster. There'd be waves of suicide, stocks collapsing, a million tragedies."

"But *after* that," the sergeant said. "After they realized it was true, that every nation was disarmed and there was nothing more to fear, if we were all clean to start over fresh and new, what then?"

"They'd rearm as swiftly as possible."

"What if they could be stopped?"

"Then they'd beat each other with their fists. If it got down to that. Huge armies of men with boxing gloves of steel spikes would gather at the national borders. And if you took the gloves away they'd use their fingernails and feet. And if you cut their legs off they'd *spit* on each other. And if you cut off their tongues and stopped their mouths with corks they'd fill the atmosphere so full of hate that mosquitoes would drop to the ground and birds would fall dead from telephone wires."

"Then you don't think it would do any good?" the sergeant said.

"Certainly not. It'd be like ripping the carapace off a turtle. Civilization would gasp and die from the shock."

The young man shook his head. "Or are you lying to yourself and me because you've a nice comfortable job?"

"Let's call it ninety per cent cynicism, ten per cent rationalizing the situation. Go put your Rust away and forget about it."

The sergeant jerked his head up. "How'd you know I *had* it?" he said.

"Had what?"

"The Rust, of course."

"What're you talking about?"

"I *can* do it, you know. I could start the Rust tonight if I wanted to."

The Official laughed. "You can't be serious."

"I am. I've been meaning to come talk to you. I'm glad you called me in. I've worked on this invention for a long time. It's been a dream of mine. It has to do with the structure of certain atoms. If you study them you find that the arrangement of atoms in steel armor is such-and-such an arrangement. I was looking for an imbalance factor. I majored in physics and metallurgy, you know. It came to me, there's a Rust factor in the air all the time. Water vapor. I had to find a way to give steel a 'nervous breakdown.' Then the water vapor everywhere in the world would take over. Not on all metal, of course. Our civilization is built on steel, I wouldn't want to destroy most buildings. I'd just eliminate guns and shells, tanks, planes, battleships. I can set the machine to work on copper and brass and aluminum, too, if necessary. I'd just walk by all of those weapons and just being near them I'd make them fall away."

The Official was bending over his desk, staring at the sergeant. "May I ask you a question?"

"Yes."

"Have you ever thought you were Christ?"

"I can't say that I have. But I have considered that God was good to me to let me find what I was looking for, if that's what you mean."

The Official reached into his breast pocket and drew out an expensive ball-point pen capped with a rifle shell. He flourished the pen and started filling in a form. "I want you to take this to Dr Mathews this afternoon, for a complete check-up. Not that I expect anything really bad, understand. But don't you feel you *should* see a doctor?"

"You think I'm lying about my machine," said the sergeant. "I'm not. It's so small it can be hidden in this cigarette package. The effect of it extends for nine hundred miles. I could tour this country in a few days, with the machine set to a certain type of steel. The other nations couldn't take advantage of us because I'd rust their weapons as they approach us. Then I'd fly to Europe. By this time next month the world would be free of war forever. I don't know how I found this invention. It's impossible. Just as impossible as the atom bomb. I've waited a month now, trying to think it over. I worried about what would happen if I did rip off the carapace, as you say. But now I've just about decided. My talk with you has helped clarify things. Nobody thought an aeroplane would ever fly, nobody thought an atom would ever explode, and nobody thinks that there can ever be Peace, but there *will* be."

"Take that paper over to Dr Mathews, will you?" said the Official hastily.

The sergeant got up. "You're not going to assign me to any new Zone then?"

"Not right away, no. I've changed my mind. We'll let Mathews decide."

"I've decided then," said the young man. "I'm leaving the Post within the next few minutes. I've a pass. Thank you very much for giving me your valuable time, sir."

"Now look here, Sergeant, don't take things so seriously. You don't have to leave. Nobody's going to hurt you."

"That's right. Because nobody would believe me. Goodbye, sir." The sergeant opened the office door and stepped out.

The door shut and the Official was alone. He stood for a moment looking at the door. He sighed. He rubbed his hands over his face. The phone rang. He answered it abstractedly.

"Oh, *hello*, Doctor. I was just going to call you." A pause. "Yes, I was going to send him over to you. Look, is it all right for that young man to be wandering about? It *is* all right? If you say so, Doctor. Probably needs a rest, a good long one. Poor boy has a delusion of rather an interesting sort. Yes, yes. It's a shame. But that's what a Sixteen-Year War can do to you, I suppose."

The phone voice buzzed in reply.

The Official listened and nodded. "I'll make a note on that. Just a second." He reached for his ball-point pen. "Hold on a moment. Always mislaying things." He patted his pocket. "Had my pen here a moment ago. Wait." He put down the phone and searched his desk, pulling out drawers. He checked his blouse pocket again. He stopped moving. Then his hands twitched slowly into his pocket and probed down. He poked his thumb and forefinger deep and brought out a pinch of something.

He sprinkled it on his desk blotter: a small filtering powder of yellow-red rust.

He sat staring at it for a moment. Then he picked up the phone. "Mathews," he said, "get off the line, quick." There was a click of someone hanging up and then he dialed another call. "Hello, Guard Station, listen, there's a man coming past you any minute now, you know him, name of Sergeant Hollis, stop him, shoot him down, kill him if necessary, don't ask any questions, kill the son of a bitch, you heard me, this is the Official talking! Yes, kill him, you hear!"

"But, sir," said a bewildered voice on the other end of the line. "I can't, I just *can't* . . ."

"What do you mean you can't, God damn it!"

"Because . . ." The voice faded away. You could hear the guard breathing into the phone a mile away.

The Official shook the phone. "Listen to me, listen, get your gun ready!"

"I can't shoot anyone," said the guard.

The Official sank back in his chair. He sat blinking for half a minute, gasping.

Out there even now – he didn't have to look, no one had to tell him – the hangars were dusting down in soft red rust, and the aeroplanes were blowing away on a brownrust wind into nothingness, and the tanks were sinking, sinking slowly into the hot asphalt roads, like dinosaurs (isn't that what the man had said?) sinking into primordial tar pits. Trucks were blowing away into ochre puffs of smoke, their drivers dumped by the road, with only the tires left running on the highways.

"Sir . . ." said the guard, who was seeing all this, far away. "Oh, God . . ."

"Listen, listen!" screamed the Official. "Go after him, get him, with your hands, choke him, with your fists, beat him, use your feet, kick his ribs in, kick him to death, do anything, but get that man. I'll be right out!" He hung up the phone.

By instinct he jerked open the bottom desk drawer to get his service pistol. A pile of brown rust filled the new leather holster. He swore and leaped up.

On the way out of the office he grabbed a chair. It's wood, he thought. Good old-fashioned wood, good old-fashioned maple. He hurled it against the wall twice, and it broke. Then he seized one of the legs, clenched it hard in his fist, his face bursting red, the breath snorting in his nostrils, his mouth wide. He struck the palm of his hand with the leg of the chair, testing it. "All right, God damn it, come on!" he cried.

He rushed out, yelling, and slammed the door.

Biographical Notes

Ray Bradbury was born in Illinois, in 1920. While still at High School, he began to write stories of fantasy, reflecting his childhood interest in circuses, magicians, thought readers, etc., and his avid consumption of sensational literature and comics. After leaving school he continued to write, earning his living on the side as a newspaper vendor.

On his twenty-first birthday he was surprised by the publication of one of his stories in a popular magazine. Soon his stories began appearing in quality magazines, and several were included in the annual anthologies Best American Short Stories. *His most successful works are the sequence of short stories published as* The Martian Chronicles *(1950), and the novel* Fahrenheit 451 *(1951). The latter was turned into a film (directed by François Truffaut) in 1966.*

In almost all of his stories, Ray Bradbury can be said to use the form of science fiction as a vehicle for reflection about present tendencies.

Annotations

19 13 **casing** protective metallic covering – 17 **chatter** *(n.)* foolish talk – 22 **flaking** with bits falling off the surface – 27 **suicide** ['su:ɪsaɪd] act of killing oneself – **stocks collapsing** shares in a company (Aktien) losing their value – 32 **swift** quick, fast

20 9 **to rip off** to remove s.th. quickly and violently – **carapace** ['kærəpeɪs] hard shell on the back of certain animals – **turtle** Schildkröte – 13 **to rationalize** to find reasonable-sounding explanations for – 15 **to jerk** to make a short, quick movement – 24 **armo(u)r** ['ɑ:mə] strong protective covering – 25 **to major in** *Am.* to study as a main subject – 27 **vapo(u)r** ['veɪpə] gas, steam – 30 **to eliminate** to do away with – **shell** metal case filled with explosives – 31 **brass** hard yellow metal made by mixing copper and zinc

21 2 **to flourish** ['flʌrɪʃ] to wave in a showy manner – 7 **to extend** to reach – 20 **to assign** [ə'saɪn] to give a particular job or position to s.o. – 23 **the Post** *here:* the military camp – 32 **abstractedly** lost in thought – 36 **delusion** false belief

22 3 **to mislay** to lose – 6 **to twitch** to make short, sharp movements – **to probe** to search – **to poke** to push into – 7 **pinch** very small amount of s.th. (Prise) – 8 **blotter** piece of thick soft paper for drying ink – 15 **son of a bitch** *Am. vulg.* term of abuse, like 'bastard' – 17 **bewildered** [bɪ'wɪldəd] confused, puzzled – 24 **to blink** (of eyes) to open and shut quickly – 27 **hangar** building in which aeroplanes are kept – 30 **primordial** [praɪ'mɔ:dɪəl] existing from the earliest times – 31 **ochre** ['əʊkə] brownish-yellow – 35 **to choke** to stop s.o. breathing – 39 **to swear** ['sweə] **swore, sworn** to express one's anger through the use of vulgar language

23 2 **maple** [eɪ] type of northern tree with pointed leaves (Ahorn) – **to hurl** to throw with great force – 3 **to seize** [i:] to take hold of – **to clench** to hold firmly – 4 **to snort** to blow air through one's nose – 7 **to yell** to shout

Liam O'Flaherty

His First Flight

The young seagull was alone on his ledge. His two brothers and his sister had already flown away the day before. He had been afraid to fly with them. Somehow when he had taken a little run forward to the brink of the ledge and attempted to flap his wings he became afraid. The great expanse of sea stretched down beneath, and it was such a long way down – miles down. He felt certain that his wings would never support him, so he bent his head and ran away back to the little hole under the ledge where he slept at night. Even when each of his brothers and his little sister, whose wings were far shorter than his own, ran to the brink, flapped their wings, and flew away he failed to muster up courage to take that plunge which appeared to him so desperate. His father and mother had come around calling to him shrilly, upbraiding him, threatening to let him starve on his ledge unless he flew away. But for the life of him he could not move.

That was twenty-four hours ago. Since then nobody had come near him. The day before, all day long, he had watched his parents flying about with his brothers and sister, perfecting them in the art of flight, teaching them how to skim the waves and how to dive for fish. He had, in fact, seen his older brother catch his first herring and devour it, standing on a rock, while his parents circled around raising a proud cackle. And all the morning the whole family had walked about on the big plateau midway down the opposite cliff, taunting him with his cowardice.

The sun was now ascending the sky, blazing warmly on his ledge that faced the south. He felt the heat because he had not eaten since the previous nightfall. Then he had found a dried piece of mackerel's tail at the far end of his ledge. Now there was not a single scrap of food left. He had searched every inch, rooting among the rough, dirt-caked straw nest where he and his brothers and sister had been hatched. He even gnawed at the dried pieces of spotted eggshell. It was like eating part of himself. He had then trotted back and forth from one end of the ledge to the other, his grey body the colour of the cliff, his long grey legs stepping daintily, trying to find some means of reaching his parents without having to fly. But on each side of him the ledge ended in a sheer fall of precipice, with the sea beneath. And between him and his parents there was a deep, wide chasm. Surely he could reach them without flying if he could only move northwards along the cliff face? But then on what could he walk? There was no ledge, and he was not a fly. And above him he could see nothing. The precipice was sheer, and the top of it was perhaps farther away than the sea beneath him.

He stepped slowly out to the brink of the ledge, and, standing on one leg with the other leg hidden under his wing, he closed one eye, then the other, and pretended to be falling asleep. Still they took no notice of him. He saw his two brothers and his sister lying on the plateau dozing, with their heads sunk into their necks. His father was preening the feathers on his white back. Only his mother was looking at him. She was standing on a little high hump on the plateau, her white breast thrust forward. Now and again she tore at a piece of fish that lay at her feet, and then scraped each side of her beak on the rock. The sight of the food maddened him. How he loved to tear food that way, scraping his beak now and again to whet it! He uttered a low cackle. His mother cackled too, and looked over at him.

"Ga, ga, ga," he cried, begging her to bring him over some food. "Gaw-ool-ah," she screamed back derisively. But he kept calling plaintively, and after a minute or so he uttered a joyful scream. His mother had picked up a piece of the fish and was flying across to him with it. He leaned out eagerly, tapping the rock with his feet, trying to get nearer to her as she flew across. But when she was just opposite to him, abreast of the ledge, she halted, her legs hanging limp, her wings motionless, the piece of fish in her beak almost within reach of his beak. He waited a moment in surprise, wondering why she did not come nearer, and then, maddened by hunger, he dived at the fish. With a loud scream he fell outwards and downwards into space. His mother had swooped upwards. As he passed beneath her he heard the swish of her wings. Then a monstrous terror seized him and his heart stood still. He could hear nothing. But it only lasted a moment. The next moment he felt his wings spread outwards. The wind rushed against his breast feathers, then under his stomach and against his wings. He could feel the tips of his wings cutting through the air. He was not falling headlong now. He was soaring gradually downwards and outwards. He was no longer afraid. He just felt a bit dizzy. Then he flapped his wings once and he soared upwards. He uttered a joyous scream and flapped them again. He soared higher. He raised his breast and banked against the wind. "Ga, ga, ga. Ga, ga, ga. Gaw-ool-ah." His mother swooped past him, her wings making a loud noise. He answered her with another scream. Then his father flew over him screaming. Then he saw his two brothers and his sister flying around him curveting and banking and soaring and diving.

Then he completely forgot that he had not always been able to fly, and commenced himself to dive and soar and curvet, shrieking shrilly.

He was near the sea now, flying straight over it, facing straight out over the ocean. He saw a vast green sea beneath him, with little ridges moving over it, and he turned his beak sideways and crowed amusedly. His parents and his brothers and sister had landed on this green floor in front of him. They were beckoning to him, calling shrilly. He dropped his legs to stand on the green sea. His legs sank into it. He screamed with fright and attempted to rise again, flapping his wings. But he was tired and weak with hunger and he could not rise, exhausted by the strange exercise. His feet sank into the green sea, and then his belly touched it and he sank no farther. He was floating on it. And around him his family was screaming, praising him, and their beaks were offering him scraps of dog-fish.

He had made his first flight.

Biographical Notes

Liam O'Flaherty was born in 1897 on the main island of the Aran group off the west coast of Ireland. He was the ninth of ten children who all had to be supported on fifteen acres of rocky land. Gaelic was his native language but he soon started to learn English.

At the age of 13 he was educated for the priesthood at two secondary schools on the mainland which were run by the Holy Ghost Fathers. A few years later, however, he decided against becoming a priest and got a scholarship to study Greek and Latin at University College, Dublin.

At the beginning of the First World War he joined the Irish Guards and fought in France. He returned wounded to the Aran Islands in 1917. The following years he spent travelling widely in Europe and America, earning his living as a stoker, a miner, a lumberjack, and a dock labourer. In 1922 he was back in Ireland and fought in the Civil War on the radical Republican side. Fearing arrest, he escaped to London and there started to write.

Liam O'Flaherty caught the public's attention with his vivid description of the revolutionary war in his short novel, The Informer *(1926). This was made into a Hollywood film directed by John Ford (1935). His other novels,* Skerett *(1932) and* Famine *(1937), are generally considered to be even more successful, in literary terms.*

His great narrative talent also showed in numerous tales of country life, collected in the volumes Spring Sowing *(1924),* The Tent *(1926), and* The Mountain Tavern *(1929). O'Flaherty's ability to observe and identify with nature is unequalled among European writers. This aspect of his art comes out very clearly in the story we have chosen.*

Annotations

25 1 **ledge** narrow, flat shelf coming out from a wall or cliff – 3 **brink** edge at the top of a cliff – 4 **expanse** [–'–] large open area – 10 **to muster courage** to overcome one's fear – **plunge** jump downwards, dive – 12 **to upbraid** to scold, to speak angrily to s.o. – 17 **to skim** to move near the surface, barely touching it – 18 **to devour** [dɪ'vaʊə] to eat up quickly and hungrily – 19 **cackle** sound like that made by a hen – 21 **to taunt** [ɔ:] to try to make s.o. angry by laughing at his faults – **cowardice** ['kaʊədɪs] lack of courage – 22

to ascend [–'–] to get higher – **to blaze** to burn brightly – 25 **scrap** small piece – 27 **to hatch** to make a young bird break through the eggshell – **to gnaw** [nɔ:] to keep biting s.th. hard – 30 **daintily** *here:* stiffly and over-anxiously – 32 **sheer** straight down – **precipice** ['presɪpɪs] steep face of rock – 33 **chasm** ['kæzm] very deep hole

26 8 **to doze** to be half asleep – 9 **to preen** to arrange (feathers) with the beak – 11 **to thrust** to push forward – 13 **beak** a bird's hard and horny mouth – 14 **to whet** to sharpen – 17 **derisively** in a mocking way, laughing at s.o.'s foolishness – **plaintively** in a sad way – 21 **abreast of** on a level with – 22 **limp** loose, not stiff – 26 **to swoop** to rush through the air – 31 **headlong** without control – 32 **to soar** to sail through the air – 33 **dizzy** feeling as if everything were turning round – 35 **to bank (against)** to fly with one side higher than the other – 39 **to curvet** [kɜ:'vet] *here:* to keep changing direction

27 2 **to commence** to begin, to start – **to shriek** [i:] to scream – 4 **ridges** *here:* the long, white tops of the waves – 7 **to beckon** to signal to s.o. to come nearer – 10 **exhausted** very tired – 11 **belly** *here:* the underside of an animal's body

Shirley Jackson

Charles

The day my son Laurie started kindergarten he renounced corduroy overalls with bibs and began wearing blue jeans with a belt. I watched him go off the first morning with the older girl next door, seeing clearly that an era of my life was ended, my sweet-voiced nursery-school tot replaced by a long-trousered, swaggering character who forgot to stop at the corner and wave good-bye to me.

He came home the same way, the front door slamming open, his hat on the floor, and the voice suddenly become raucous, shouting, "Isn't anybody *here*?"

At lunch he spoke insolently to his father, spilled his baby sister's milk, and remarked that his teacher said we were not to take the name of the Lord in vain.

"How *was* school today?" I asked, elaborately casual.

"All right," he said.

"Did you learn anything?" his father asked.

Laurie regarded his father coldly. "I didn't learn nothing," he said.

"Anything," I said. "Didn't learn anything."

"The teacher spanked a boy, though," Laurie said, addressing his bread and butter. "For being fresh," he added, with his mouth full.

"What did he do?" I asked. "Who was it?"

Laurie thought. "It was Charles," he said. "He was fresh. The teacher spanked him and made him stand in a corner. He was awfully fresh."

"What did he do?" I asked again, but Laurie slid off his chair, took a cookie, and left, while his father was still saying, "See here, young man."

The next day Laurie remarked at lunch, as soon as he sat down, "Well, Charles was bad again today." He grinned enormously and said, "Today Charles hit the teacher."

"Good heavens," I said, mindful of the Lord's name. "I suppose he got spanked again?"

"He sure did," Laurie said. "Look up," he said to his father.

"What?" his father said, looking up.

"Look down," Laurie said. "Look at my thumb. Gee, you're dumb." He began to laugh insanely.

"Why did Charles hit the teacher?" I asked quickly.

"Because she tried to make him color with red crayons," Laurie said. "Charles wanted to color with green crayons so he hit the teacher and she spanked him and said nobody play with Charles but everybody did."

The third day – it was Wednesday of the first week – Charles bounced a see-saw on the head of a little girl and made her bleed, and the teacher made him stay inside all during recess. Thursday Charles had to stand in a corner during story-time because he kept pounding his feet on the floor. Friday Charles was deprived of blackboard privileges because he threw chalk.

On Saturday I remarked to my husband, "Do you think kindergarten is too unsettling for Laurie? All this toughness and bad grammar, and this Charles boy sounds like such a bad influence."

"It'll be all right," my husband said reassuringly. "Bound to be people like Charles in the world. Might as well meet them now as later."

On Monday Laurie came home late, full of news. "Charles," he shouted as he came up the hill; I was waiting anxiously on the front steps. "Charles," Laurie yelled all the way up the hill, "Charles was bad again."

"Come right in," I said, as soon as he came close enough. "Lunch is waiting."

"You know what Charles did?" he demanded, following me through the door. "Charles yelled so in school they sent a boy in from first grade to tell the teacher she had to make Charles keep quiet, and so Charles had to stay after school. And so all the children stayed to watch him."

"What did he do?" I asked.

"He just sat there," Laurie said, climbing into his chair at the table. "Hi, Pop, y'old dust mop."

"Charles had to stay after school today," I told my husband. "Everyone stayed with him."

"What does this Charles look like?" my husband asked Laurie. "What's his other name?"

"He's bigger than me," Laurie said. "And he doesn't have any rubbers and he doesn't ever wear a jacket."

Monday night was the first Parent-Teachers meeting, and only the fact that the baby had a cold kept me from going; I wanted passionately to meet Charles' mother. On Tuesday Laurie remarked suddenly, "Our teacher had a friend come to see her in school today."

"Charles's mother?" my husband and I asked simultaneously.

"Naaah," Laurie said scornfully. "It was a man who came and made us do exercises, we had to touch our toes. Look." He climbed down from his chair and squatted down and touched his toes. "Like this," he said. He got solemnly back into his chair and said, picking up his fork, "Charles didn't even *do* exercises."

"That's fine," I said heartily. "Didn't Charles want to do the exercises?"

"Naaah," Laurie said. "Charles was so fresh to the teacher's friend he wasn't *let* do exercises."

"Fresh again," I said.

"He kicked the teacher's friend," Laurie said. "The teacher's friend told Charles to touch his toes like I just did and Charles kicked him."

"What are they going to do about Charles, do you suppose?" Laurie's father asked him.

Laurie shrugged elaborately. "Throw him out of school, I guess," he said.

Wednesday and Thursday were routine; Charles yelled during story hour and hit a boy in the stomach and made him cry. On Friday Charles stayed after school again and so did all the other children.

With the third week of kindergarten Charles was an institution in our family; the baby was being a Charles when he filled his wagon full of mud and pulled it through the kitchen; even my husband, when he caught his elbow in the telephone cord and pulled telephone, ashtray, and a bowl of flowers off the table, said, after the first minute, "Looks like Charles."

During the third and fourth weeks it looked like a reformation in Charles; Laurie reported grimly at lunch on Thursday of the third week, "Charles was so good today the teacher gave him an apple."

"What?" I said, and my husband added warily, "You mean Charles?"

"Charles," Laurie said. "He gave the crayons around and he picked up the books afterward and the teacher said he was her helper."

"What happened?" I asked incredulously.

"He was her helper, that's all," Laurie said, and shrugged.

"Can this be true, about Charles?" I asked my husband that night. "Can something like this happen?"

"Wait and see," my husband said cynically. "When you've got a Charles to deal with, this may mean he's only plotting."

He seemed to be wrong. For over a week Charles was the teacher's helper; each day he handed things out and he picked things up; no one had to stay after school.

"The PTA meeting's next week again," I told my husband one evening. "I'm going to find Charles's mother there."

"Ask her what happened to Charles," my husband said. "I'd like to know."

"I'd like to know myself," I said.

On Friday of that week things were back to normal. "You know what Charles did today?" Laurie demanded at the lunch table, in a voice slightly awed. "He told a little girl to say a word and she said it and the teacher washed her mouth out with soap and Charles laughed."

"What word?" his father asked unwisely, and Laurie said, "I'll have to whisper it to you, it's so bad." He got down off his chair and went around to his father. His father bent his head down and Laurie whispered joyfully. His father's eyes widened.

"Did Charles tell the little girl to say *that*?" he asked respectfully.

"She said it *twice,*" Laurie said. "Charles told her to say it *twice.*"

"What happened to Charles?" my husband asked.

"Nothing," Laurie said. "He was passing out the crayons."

Monday morning Charles abandoned the little girl and said the evil word himself three or four times, getting his mouth washed out with soap each time. He also threw chalk.

My husband came to the door with me that evening as I set out for the PTA meeting. "Invite her over for a cup of tea after the meeting," he said. "I want to get a look at her."

"If only she's there," I said prayerfully.

"She'll be there," my husband said. "I don't see how they could hold a PTA meeting without Charles's mother."

At the meeting I sat restlessly, scanning each comfortable matronly face, trying to determine which one hid the secret of Charles. None of them looked to me haggard enough. No one stood up in the meeting and apologized for the way her son had been acting. No one mentioned Charles.

After the meeting I identified and sought out Laurie's kindergarten teacher. She had a plate with a cup of tea and a piece of chocolate cake; I had a plate with a cup of tea and a piece of marshmallow cake. We maneuvered up to one another cautiously, and smiled.

"I've been so anxious to meet you," I said. "I'm Laurie's mother."

"We're all so interested in Laurie," she said.

"Well, he certainly likes kindergarten," I said. "He talks about it all the time."

"We had a little trouble adjusting, the first week or so," she said primly, "but now he's a fine little helper. With occasional lapses, of course."

"Laurie usually adjusts very quickly," I said. "I suppose this time it's Charles's influence."

"Charles?"

"Yes," I said, laughing, "you must have your hands full in that kindergarten, with Charles."

"Charles?" she said. "We don't have any Charles in the kindergarten."

Biographical Notes

Shirley Jackson was born in 1919 in San Francisco, where she spent most of her early life. She studied at Syracuse University, New York. After graduating with a B.A. degree in 1940, she married a well-known literary critic and settled in Vermont.

Eight years later Shirley Jackson published her first novel, The Road Through The Wall *(1948), and a collection of short stories entitled* The Lottery *(1949). The title story had caused a literary sensation when first published in* The New Yorker. *One of her later stories – a dramatic ghost story – was filmed as* The Haunting.

Most of her best-known stories deal with tragic subjects, or with surprising or even shocking developments in an everyday setting. However, the story in our collection shows that she also had a considerable gift for humour.

Shirley Jackson was mother of two daughters and two sons. She died in 1965.

Annotations

30 1 **kindergarten** *Am.* school for children aged about 5–6 – **to renounce** to give up – **overalls** trousers with the front extending above the waist – 2 **bib** *here:* top part of an apron or overalls – 4 **nursery school** school for children under 5 – **tot** very small child – 5 **to swagger** [æ] to walk in a proud and self-important way – 7 **to slam** to hit or push loudly and with force – 8 **raucous** ['rɔ:kəs] sounding rough and unpleasant or loud and rowdy – 10 **insolent** ['– – –] rude, disrespectful – **to spill** to cause a liquid to run over the side of the container – 11 **to take the name of the Lord in vain** to use God's name in a disrespectful way – 13 **elaborate** [ɪ'læbərət] with great care – **casual** ['kæʒʊəl], *here:* seeming not to care – 18 **to spank** to beat (a child) on the behind – 19 **fresh** *Am. coll.* cheeky, rude (cf. *Ger.* 'frech') – 24 **cookie** *Am.* biscuit – 28 **mindful** *here:* taking care not to use 30 – **sure** *Am. coll.* certainly – 32 **gee** [dʒi:] *Am. sl.* expression of surprise – **dumb** [dʌm] *Am. coll.* stupid (cf. *Ger.* 'dumm') – 33 **insane** mad

31 2 **crayon** ['kreɪɒn] stick of coloured wax – 5 **to bounce** *here:* to cause to move down violently – 6 **see-saw** Wippe – 7 **recess** *Am.* break between classes – 8 **to pound** to strike heavily and noisily – 9 **to deprive of** to take away from – 12 **unsettling** disturbing – **toughness** ['tʌfnəs] hard, violent behaviour – 14 **to reassure** [ˌriːə'ʃʊə] to comfort – **(there are) bound to be** there must be – 18 **to yell** to shout – 21 **grade** *Am.* form, class, year – 26 **Pop** *Am. coll.* Father, Dad – 32 **rubbers** shoes made of rubber – 35 **passionately** *here:* very much – 38 **simultaneous** at the same time – 39 **scornful** full of contempt, disrespectful – 40 **exercises** *here:* physical training

32 1 **to squat** [ɒ] to sit on one's heels – 2 **solemn** ['– –] serious, earnest – 4 **hearty** with feeling – 12 **to shrug** to raise one's shoulders as an expression of ignorance or indifference – 21 **reformation** improvement – 24 **wary** cautious, very careful – 27 **incredulous** [ɪŋ'kredjʊləs] unable to believe – 32 **to plot** to make secret plans – 36 **PTA** Parent-Teacher Association

33 3 **to awe** [ɔː] to fill with respect – 13 **to abandon** [–'– –] to give up – **evil** ['iːvəl] very bad, wicked – 19 **prayerful** like a prayer – 22 **to scan** to look at closely – **matronly** ['meɪtrənlɪ] (of a woman) middle-aged – 24 **haggard** tired from suffering of anxiety – 29 **marshmallow** soft, spongy sweet – 30 **cautious** ['kɔːʃəs] careful – 31 **to be anxious to do s.th.** to have a strong wish to do s.th. – 35 **to adjust** to get used to (new circumstances) – **prim** stiff and self-controlled – 36 **lapse** a fall back into bad habits

James Thurber

The Princess and the Tin Box

Once upon a time, in a far country, there lived a king whose daughter was the prettiest princess in the world. Her eyes were like the cornflower, her hair was sweeter than the hyacinth, and her throat made the swan look dusty.

From the time she was a year old, the princess had been showered with presents. Her nursery looked like Cartier's window. Her toys were all made of gold or platinum or diamonds or emeralds. She was not permitted to have wooden blocks or china dolls or rubber dogs or linen books, because such materials were considered cheap for the daughter of a king.

When she was seven, she was allowed to attend the wedding of her brother and throw real pearls at the bride instead of rice. Only the nightingale, with his lyre of gold, was permitted to sing for the princess. The common blackbird, with his boxwood flute, was kept out of the palace grounds. She walked in silver-and-samite slippers to a sapphire-and-topaz bathroom and slept in an ivory bed inlaid with rubies.

On the day the princess was eighteen, the king sent a royal ambassador to the courts of five neighboring kingdoms to announce that he would give his daughter's hand in marriage to the prince who brought her the gift she liked the most.

The first prince to arrive at the palace rode a swift white stallion and laid at the feet of the princess an enormous apple made of solid gold which he had taken from a dragon who had guarded it for a thousand years. It was placed on a long ebony table set up to hold the gifts of the princess's suitors. The second prince, who came on a grey charger, brought her a nightingale made of a thousand diamonds, and it was placed beside the golden apple. The third prince, riding on a black horse, carried a great jewel box made of platinum and sapphires, and it was placed next to the diamond nightingale. The fourth prince, astride a fiery yellow horse, gave the princess a gigantic heart made of rubies and pierced by an emerald arrow. It was placed next to the platinum-and-sapphire jewel box.

Now the fifth prince was the strongest and handsomest of all the five suitors, but he was the son of a poor king whose realm had been overrun by mice and locusts and wizards and mining engineers so that there was nothing much of value left in it. He came plodding up to the palace of the princess on a plow horse and he brought her a small tin box filled with mica and feldspar and hornblende which he had picked up on the way.

The other princes roared with disdainful laughter when they saw the tawdry gift the fifth prince had brought to the princess. But she examined it with great interest and squealed with delight, for all her life she had been glutted with precious stones and priceless metals, but she had never seen tin before or mica or feldspar or hornblende. The tin box was placed next to the ruby heart pierced with an emerald arrow.

"Now," the king said to his daughter, "you must select the gift you like best and marry the prince that brought it."

The princess smiled and walked up to the table and picked up the present she liked the most. It was the platinum-and-sapphire jewel box, the gift of the third prince.

"The way I figure it," she said, "is this. It is a very large and expensive box, and when I am married, I will meet many admirers who will give me precious gems with which to fill it to the top. Therefore, it is the most valuable of all the gifts my suitors have brought me and I like it the best."

The princess married the third prince that very day in the midst of great merriment and high revelry. More than a hundred thousand pearls were thrown at her and she loved it.

Moral: *All those who thought the princess was going to select the tin box filled with worthless stones instead of one of the other gifts will kindly stay after class and write one hundred times on the blackboard 'I would rather have a hunk of aluminum silicate than a diamond necklace.'*

Biographical Notes

James Thurber is considered by many to be America's greatest 20th-century humorist. He was born in Columbus, Ohio in 1894. From early childhood, he suffered from bad eyesight. He was therefore prevented from joining the army in the First World War and worked as a government clerk instead.

After graduating from Ohio State University he held a number of jobs in the U.S.A. and abroad: he was on the staff of the American Embassy in Paris for two years and then worked as a journalist for several American daily newspapers. In 1926 he joined the staff of The New Yorker *– a famous American critical and satirical magazine. It was this magazine that first published most of his stories and cartoons.*

Altogether James Thurber published twenty books, most of them a mixture of cartoons, sketches, stories and essays. One of his favourite forms was the fable – it enabled him to make subtle and satirical points about the ways of the (modern) world.

He was twice married and divorced. In his later life he lived alone in Connecticut suffering from increasing blindness. He died in New York in 1961.

Annotations

36 6 **nursery** child's playroom or bedroom – **Cartier's** expensive French jeweller's shop, with branches in large cities all over the world – 7 **platinum** ['plætɪnəm] greyish-white metal, even more expensive than gold – **emerald, sapphire, topaz, ruby** (green, blue, yellow and red) precious stones – 8 **china dolls** dolls made of china (Porzellan) – **linen books** books covered in linen (Leinen), i.e. cheaper than leather-bound ones – 11 **rice** In Britain and America, a bride and groom are showered with rice and/or confetti. – 12 **lyre** ['laɪə] very old musical instrument with strings – 13 **blackbird** ['––] singing bird with a yellow beak – **boxwood** wood of a small tree (Buchsbaum) – 14 **samite** ['sæmɪt] silk brocade – 15 **ivory** ['aɪvərɪ] a hard white substance from the tusks of elephants – **inlaid with rubies** with rubies set into the surface as a decoration – 16 **ambassador** [–'–––] high-ranking diplomat – 20 **swift** quick – **stallion** ['stæljən] male horse – 22 **dragon** ['drægən] (in stories) fire-breathing animal – 23 **ebony** ['ebəni] hard black wood – **suitor** (old use) man wishing to marry a woman – 24 **charger** (old use) horse used in battles – 28 **astride** riding on – **gigantic** [dʒaɪ'gæntɪk] – 29 **to pierce** to make a hole through s.th. – 31 **handsome** good-looking – 32 **realm** [relm] kingdom – 33 **locust** ['ləʊkəst] insect that flies in great swarms and destroys crops – **wizard** ['wɪzəd] (in stories) man who has magic powers – **mining engineer** an expert in getting minerals out of the earth (Bergbauingenieur)

37 1 **to plod** to move slowly and heavily – 2 **mica, feldspar, hornblende** worthless stones which are pretty and colourful – 4 **disdainful** showing one's low opinion of s.o./s.th. – 5 **tawdry** cheap, lacking good taste – 6 **to squeal** to make a high-pitched sound – 7 **to glut with** to give too much of – 15 **to figure** *coll.* to see, to understand – 16 **admirer** person who finds s.o./s.th. beautiful or interesting – 17 **gem** [dʒem] polished precious stone – 19 **in the midst of** in the middle of – 20 **merriment** joyful laughter – **revelry** ['– – –] dancing, singing and feasting – 25 **hunk** large, rough piece – **aluminum silicate** a component of many rocks – **necklace** ['nekləs] string of jewels worn around the neck

Lord Dunsany

The Speech

"Crime," said the old journalist one night at his club. "One reads a good deal about violence nowadays; but I never read of a crime that would make a story like the one that there was when I was young. That would have made a story. But it was all hushed up."

"No doubt for some good reason," a younger journalist said.

"Yes," said the old journalist. "It had to be. They were extremely careful not to disturb the peace of Europe in those days. That, you see, was what the crime was about. There was a young man, scarcely remembered now, brilliant though he was – the Honourable Peter Minch. His old father you would never have heard of. A totally obscure old peer, Lord Inchingthwaite. But people heard of Peter Minch in his time. He was an M.P. and the coming man of the Opposition, one of those coming men that you never hear any more of.

"At the time that I tell about, he was going to make a speech in the House. Things had been simmering for some time. What this young fellow was going to say just at that time wasn't going to help the peace of Europe at all. What he was going to say would have prodded Austria pretty hard; and, if Germany had supported her in what would have been quite justifiable resentment, Russia would not have liked it, and the fat would have been in the fire. But there was no stopping Minch. He was a bit of a firebrand. The government couldn't stop him, of course. And as for the Opposition, he was their fancy man, and they were probably thinking more of how it would embarrass the government than how it would annoy the Austrians."

And then (the old journalist went on) the extraordinary thing happened. A man walked into the central office of Minch's party, without giving his name, and said quite clearly that he had sure information that was not exactly a message, and must not be taken as a threat but only a warning, that that speech would never be made.

"What do you mean?" said the Chairman of the Party.

"I mean," said the man, "that there is an organization with which I have nothing to do, nothing whatever, who are determined to stop that speech, and who are powerful enough to do what they threaten. It is not I that threaten. I came to warn you."

"Do you mean," said the Chairman, "that they are going to use force?"

"They will use whatever is necessary," said the stranger. "We – that is, they – consider war to be the greater evil."

"War?" said the Chairman. "Who says we are making war?"

"Their information," said the stranger, "is that what Mr Minch is going to say just at this time will bring war nearer. They are well-informed, and they have told me they are convinced that causing the death of one man is preferable to the risk of disturbing the peace of Europe."

Well, as politely as possible, the Chairman told him to go to hell. And as the man left, he said, "That speech will not be delivered. Under no circumstances will it be, in the House."

The Opposition told Scotland Yard. And they took the matter up at once, and assured the Chairman of the Party that the entire police force of the metropolis would be available. Police protection on an enormous scale was given to Minch at once.

I think Scotland Yard must have known more than they ever told about the organization that was making that threat, because they said at once that the man that had called on the Chairman of the Party would have been a man named Hosken. And that's who he turned out to be. The Chairman asked them then if they would arrest him. But the chief inspector said: Better not – better leave him at large, and he might give them more information. And he did.

The Chairman of the Party was sitting in his office with a burden removed from his mind, for he felt that the police had everything well in hand, when in walked this extraordinary man again. They let him come in, because they wanted to hear what the fellow had to say. They addressed him by his name this time, and I think it gave the Chairman a little childish pleasure to imply by doing so that they knew all about him.

"Well, Mr Hosken," said the Chairman, "is there anything more that you wished to tell us?"

A faint smile from Hosken greeted the use of his name. And then he said, "Only to say that all those policemen will not enable Mr Minch to make that speech and start a debate in Parliament, while things are as they are just now abroad."

"If Mr Minch desires to speak in the House, as he has every right to do, he will certainly do so," said the Chairman.

"I have come to say," said Hosken, "that if he will put it off, so as to give things time to simmer down, the powerful organization with which a friend of mine is in touch will take no action."

"If you mean by 'things' the state of affairs in Europe, we are not concerned with them. No one in Europe can deny us free speech," said the Chairman.

"It would be an open defiance," said Hosken. "And would lead to war."

"You must understand," the Chairman said to Hosken, "that we cannot tolerate any more blackmail."

"Certainly, sir," said Hosken. "Only there will be no speech in Parliament by Mr Minch for at least a week. And, if you stop him peacefully, there will be no need for violence."

Then he smiled and walked out.

Well, that's how things were (went on the old journalist) – tension rather acute, and this fiery young man going to start a debate in the House that would put all the fat in the fire, and perhaps set it overflowing and scalding all Europe, and a powerful organization of blackmailers – for they were nothing less – determined that that debate should never take place, and that one man's murder was nothing compared to war. And against the blackmailing gang was practically the whole of the police force of the metropolis. I needn't go into the precautions taken by the police. They took them all. Minch was constantly under observation by at least two of them. I doubt if anyone was ever more watched in London.

They soon ran Hosken down, but did not arrest him. All they did was to keep him under observation. I fancy they thought that he would be more useful to them that way.

On a Wednesday morning everything was all ready. Minch was going to speak at seven that evening. His whole family were going to be there, his old father in the Peers' Gallery, and all the rest of his family in the Ladies' Gallery. The police had a cab for Minch which was entirely bulletproof, even to windows of plate glass that was over an inch thick.

Well, the precautions were more than would have been taken for moving bullion from the Bank of England. They asked Minch to be at the House by 3 o'clock.

As he and his police escort arrived, a messenger boy handed a note to the inspector in charge of the guard. He opened it and saw an anonymous note, saying: *Mr Minch will not make that speech today*. He smiled, because once inside the precincts of the Houses of Parliament murder was quite impossible.

Minch's family were to arrive at half past six. At 3 o'clock, a dull debate opened. And yet the tension was electric, for everyone present knew the threat of the gang. The dignity of Parliament was at stake, and most of the members, even on the side to which Minch was going to cause so much trouble, put that first. Slowly the tension heightened, as the hands of the clock moved round to four.

And in that heightened tension everyone seemed to know what everyone else was thinking. They knew when any speaker was intending to be funny, and all laughed quickly and nervously, even before the little joke came.

And then, at five minutes past four, a note for Mr Minch was handed by a policeman to the inspector, who passed it to the sergeant-at-arms, who went into the chamber and gave it to Minch. Minch opened it and turned white.

"My father is dead," he said to a member beside him. "He's been murdered."

"I am terribly sorry," said the other man. "What happened?"

Minch handed the note to him. His father had been shot dead in his house. The murderer has escaped.

"And your speech," said the other member. "I am afraid –"

"No," said Minch. "That can't stop me. Nobody could be sorrier than I am. But private grief is one thing, public duty another."

"But, look here," said the other member. "I mean – you're a peer."

"I'm a what?" said Minch.

"You're a peer now," said the other again.

"My God!" Minch answered.

Well, that was the end of that. The gang had done it. They attacked as any man of sense would always attack, at the weakest point, where nobody was expecting it. And nobody did think of poor old Lord Inchingthwaite. He was quite obscure. But the moment he died, Peter Minch became a peer, and could make no more speeches of any sort in the House of Commons.

And he couldn't even make his speech in the House of Lords, until he had taken his seat, and all that took time. He did make the speech at a meeting that week in what had been his constituency, but Austria took no notice of that.

"So war was averted," said the young journalist.

"Well, yes," said the old journalist. "Not that it made any difference in the end."

Biographical Notes

Edward John Moreton Drax Plunkett was born in London in 1878 into an aristocratic Anglo-Irish family. He was educated at Eton and Sandhurst military academy. When his father died in 1899 he became the 18th Baron Dunsany. In 1904 he married Lady Beatrice Villiers, daughter of the Earl of Jersey.

Lord Dunsany fought in the Boer War (1899–1902) and in the First World War. His literary career began between these two wars. Together with W. B. Yeats he worked for the revival of the Irish theatre and one of his first plays, The Glittering Gates, *was produced by the Abbey Theatre, Dublin, in 1909. Later his plays were also produced by the Moscow Art Theatre as well as in England and America. He became Professor of English Literature in Athens, where he remained until the Germans occupied Greece in 1941. Back in Dublin and London, Lord Dunsany became a very prolific writer, producing numerous poems and stories for publication in the daily newspapers. The list of his literary works is a long one – in all, he had well over fifty books published.*

He travelled a lot, but most of his time he spent at his home, Dunsany Castle in County Meath, Ireland, or on his English estate, Dunstall Priory, in Kent. He died in Dublin in 1957.

Annotations

40 4 **to hush s.th. up** to prevent s.th. from becoming known to the public – 9 **the Honourable** title of a son or daughter of a Lord – 10 **obscure** not well known – **peer** nobleman entitled to sit in the House of Lords – 11 **M.P.** Member of Parliament – 15 **in the House** in the House of Commons – **to simmer** *here:* to be in a state of tension – 17 **to prod** *here:* to provoke – 18 **justifiable** with good reason, understandable – 19 **resentment** feeling of anger or bitterness after one has been treated badly – **the fat would have been in the fire** things would have been made much worse – 20 **firebrand** person who stirs up political quarrels; agitator – 22 **fancy man** a man who is useful for making a good impression on the public – 23 **to embarrass** [–ˈ––] to make s.o. feel uncomfortable, to put in an awkward position – 24 **extraordinary** very unusual – 27 **threat** [θret] statement that one will harm or do violence to s.o. – 29 **chairman** someone in charge of a meeting; *here:* leader

41 3 **evil** ['i:vəl] *(n.)* s.th. very bad; disaster, misfortune – 10 **to deliver a speech** to make a speech – **under no circumstances** never, not at all – 13 **entire** complete, the whole – 14 **metropolis** large city, London – **on an enormous scale** much more than was usual – 21 **at large** free, uncontrolled, at liberty – 23 **burden** heavy load – 27 **to imply** [ɪm'plaɪ] to express indirectly – 31 **faint** weak – 37 **to put s.th. off** to delay s.th.; to decide to do s.th. at a later date – 38 **to simmer down** *here:* to become less exciting – 39 **in touch** in contact

42 2 **to deny s.o. s.th.** to refuse to give – 4 **defiance** [–'– –] action showing lack of respect for s.o.'s authority – 6 **blackmail** *here:* attempt to influence a person's behaviour by threatening violence – 11 **tension** state of excitement; feeling that something terrible is going to happen – 13 **to scald** to burn (with hot liquid) – 18 **to go into** to explain all the details of – **precautions** steps taken to avoid a possible danger – 21 **to run s.o. down** *here:* to look for and find – 27 **cab** taxi – **bulletproof** able to stop bullets (kugelsicher) – 30 **bullion** [ʊ] bars of gold or silver – 35 **inside the precincts** ['pri:sɪŋkts] within the walls – 39 **at stake** at risk, in danger

43 1 **to put s.th. first** to give most importance to – **to heighten** ['haɪtn] to become greater; to rise – 7 **sergeant-at-arms** *here:* officer whose duty it is to keep order – 16 **grief** great sorrow – 22 **any man of sense** any clear-thinking man/person – 29 **constituency** [–'– – – –] district that sends representatives to Parliament (Wahlkreis) – 31 **to avert** [ə'vɜ:t] to prevent, to stop from happening

Robert Turner

Christmas Gift

There was no snow and the temperature was a mild sixty-eight degrees and in some of the yards nearby the shrubbery was green, along with the palm trees, but still you knew it was Christmas Eve. Doors on the houses along the street held wreaths, some of them lighted. A lot of windows were lighted with red, green and blue lights. Through some of them you could see the lighted glitter of Christmas trees. Then, of course there was the music, which you could hear coming from some of the houses, the old familiar songs, *White Christmas, Ave Maria, Silent Night.*

All of that should have been fine, because Christmas in a Florida city is like Christmas any place else, a good time, a tender time. Even if you're a cop. Even if you pulled duty Christmas Eve and can't be home with your own wife and kid. But not necessarily if you're a cop on duty with four others and you're going to have to grab an escaped con and send him back, or more probably have to kill him because he was a lifer and just won't *go* back.

In the car with me was McKee, a Third-Grade, only away from a beat a few months. Young, clear-eyed, rosy-cheeked. All-American boy type and very, very serious about his work. Which was fine; which was the way you should be. We were parked about four houses down from the rented house where Mrs Bogen and her three children were living.

At the same distance the other side of the house was a sedan in which sat Lieutenant Mortell and Detective First-Grade Thrasher. Mortell was a bitter-mouthed, needlethin man, middle-aged and with very little human expression left in his eyes. He was in charge. Thrasher was a plumpish, ordinary guy, an ordinary cop.

On the street in back of the Bogen house, was another precinct car, with two other Firsts in it, a couple of guys named Dodey and Fischman. They were back there in case Earl Bogen got away from us and took off through some yards to that other block. I didn't much think he'd get to do that.

After a while McKee said: "I wonder if it's snowing up north. I'll bet the hell it is." He shifted his position. "It don't really seem like Christmas, no snow. Christmas with palm trees, what a deal!"

"That's the way it was with the first one," I reminded him.

He thought about that. Then he said: "Yeah. Yeah. That's right. But I still don't like it."

I started to ask him why he stayed down here, then I remembered about his mother. She needed the climate; it was all that kept her alive.

"Y'know," McKee said then. "Sarge, I been thinking; this guy Bogen must be nuts."

"You mean because he's human? Because he wants to see his wife and kids on Christmas?"

"Well, he must know there's a *chance* he'll be caught. If he is, it'll be worse for his wife and kids, won't it? Why the hell couldn't he just have *sent* them presents or something and then called them on the phone? Huh?"

"You're not married, are you, McKee?"

"No."

"And you don't have kids of your own. So I can't answer that question for you."

"I still think he's nuts."

I didn't answer. I was thinking how I could hound the stinking stoolie who had tipped us about Earl Bogen's visit home for Christmas, all next year, without getting into trouble. There was a real rat in my book, a guy who would stool on something like that. I was going to give him a bad time if it broke me.

Then I thought about what Lieutenant Mortell had told me an hour ago. "Tim," he said. "I'm afraid you're not a very good cop. You're too sentimental. You ought to know by now a cop can't be sentimental. Was Bogen sentimental when he crippled for life that manager of the finance company he stuck up on his last hit? Did he worry about *that* guy's wife and kids? Stop being a damned fool, will you, Tim?"

That was the answer I got to my suggestion that we let Earl Bogen get in and see his family and have his Christmas and catch him on the way out. What was there to lose, I'd said. Give the guy a break, I'd said. I'd known, of course, that Mortell wouldn't have any part of that, but I'd had to try anyhow. Even though I knew the lieutenant would think of the same thing I had – that when it came time to go, Bogen might be twice as hard to take.

McKee's bored young voice cut into my thoughts: "You think he'll really be armed? Bogen, I mean."

"I think so."

"I'm glad Mortell told us not to take any chances with him, that if he even makes a move that looks like he's going for a piece, we give it to him. He's a smart old cop, Mortell."

"That's what they say. But did you ever look at his eyes?"

"What's the matter with his eyes?" McKee said.

"Skip it," I said. "A bus has stopped."

We knew Earl Bogen had no car; we doubted he'd rent one or take a cab. He was supposed to be short of dough. A city bus from town stopped up at the corner. When he came he'd be on that, most likely. But he wasn't on this one. A lone woman got off and turned up the Avenue. I let out a slight sigh and looked at the radium dial of my watch. Ten-fifty. Another hour and ten minutes and we'd be relieved; it wouldn't happen on our tour. I hoped that was the way it would be. It was possible. The stoolie could have been wrong about the whole thing. Or something could have happened to change Bogen's plans, or at least to postpone his visit to the next day. I settled back to wait for the next bus.

McKee said: "Have you ever killed a guy, Sarge?"

"No," I said. "I never had to. But I've been there when someone else did."

"Yeah? What's it like?" McKee's voice took on an edge of excitement. "I mean for the guy who did the shooting? How'd he feel about it?"

"I don't know. I didn't ask him. But I'll tell you how he looked. He looked as though he was going to be sick to his stomach, as though he should've been but couldn't be."

"Oh," McKee said. He sounded disappointed.

"How about the guy that was shot? What'd he do? I've never seen a guy shot."

"Him?" I said. "Oh, he screamed."

"Screamed?"

"Yeah. Did you ever hear a child scream when it's had a door slammed on its fingers? That's how he screamed. He got shot in the groin."

"Oh, I see," McKee said, but he didn't sound as though he really did. I thought that McKee was going to be what they called a good cop – a nice, sane, completely insensitive type guy. For the millionth time I told myself that I ought to get out. Not after tonight's tour, not next month, next week, tomorrow, but right now. It would be the best Christmas present in the world I could give myself and my family. And at the same time I knew I never would do that. I didn't know exactly why. Fear of not being able to make a living outside; fear of winding up a burden to everybody in my old age the way my father was – those were some reasons but not the whole thing. If I talk about how after being a cop so long it gets in your blood no matter how you hate it, that sounds phony. And it would sound even worse if I said one reason I stuck was in hopes that I could make up for some of the others, that I could do some good sometimes.

"If I get to shoot Bogen," McKee said, "he won't scream."

"Why not?"

"You know how I shoot. At close range like that, I'll put one right through his eye."

"Sure, you will," I told him. "Except that you won't have the chance. We'll get him, quietly. We don't want any shooting in a neighborhood like this on Christmas Eve."

Then we saw the lights of the next bus stop up at the corner. A man and a woman got off. The woman turned up the Avenue. The man, medium height but very thin, and his arms loaded with packages, started up the street.

"Here he comes," I said. "Get out of the car, McKee."

We both got out, one on each side. The man walking toward us from the corner couldn't see us. The street was heavily shaded by strings of Australian pine planted along the walk.

"McKee," I said. "You know what the orders are. When we get up to him, Thrasher will reach him first and shove his gun into Bogen's back. Then you grab his hands and get the cuffs on him fast. I'll be back a few steps covering you. Mortell'll be behind Thrasher, covering him. You got it?"

"Right," McKee said.

We kept walking, first hurrying a little, then slowing down some, so that we'd come up to Bogen, who was walking toward us, just right, before he reached the house where his family was but not before he'd passed Mortell and Thrasher's car.

When we were only a few yards from Bogen, he passed through an open space, where the thin slice of moon filtered down through tree branches. Bogen wore no hat, just a sport jacket and shirt and slacks. He was carrying about six packages, none of them very large but all of them wrapped with gaudily colored paper, foil and ribbon. Bogen's hair was crew-cut, instead of long the way it was in police pictures and he'd grown a mustache; but none of that was much of a disguise.

Just then he saw us and hesitated in his stride. Then he stopped. Thrasher, right behind him, almost bumped into him. I heard Thrasher's bull-froggy voice say: "Drop those packages and put your hands up, Bogen. Right now!"

He dropped the packages. They tumbled about his feet on the sidewalk and two of them split open. A toy racing car was in one of them. It must have been still slightly wound up because when it broke out of the package, the little motor whirred and the tiny toy car spurted across the sidewalk two or three feet. From the other package, a small doll fell and lay on its back on the sidewalk, its big, painted eyes staring upward. It was what they call a picture doll, I think; anyhow, it was dressed like a bride. From one of the other packages a liquid began to trickle out onto the sidewalk and I figured that had been a bottle of Christmas wine for Bogen and his wife.

But when Bogen dropped the packages, he didn't raise his hands. He spun around and the sound of his elbow hitting Thrasher's face was a sickening one. Then I heard Thrasher's gun go off as he squeezed the trigger in a reflex action, but the flash from his gun was pointed at the sky.

I raised my own gun just as Bogen reached inside his jacket but I never got to use it. McKee used his. Bogen's head went back as though somebody had jolted him under the chin with the heel of a hand. He staggered backward, twisted and fell.

I went up to Bogen with my flash. The bullet from McKee's gun had entered Bogen's right eye and there was nothing there now but a horrible hole. I moved the flash beam just for a moment, I couldn't resist it, to McKee's face. The kid looked very white but his eyes were bright with excitement and he didn't look sick at all. He kept licking his lips, nervously. He kept saying: "He's dead. You don't have to be worrying about him, now. He's dead."

Front door lights began to go on then in nearby houses and people began coming out of them. Mortell shouted to them: "Go on back inside. There's nothing to see. Police business. Go on back inside."

Of course, most of them didn't do that. They came and looked, although we didn't let them get near the body. Thrasher radioed back to Headquarters. Mortell told me: "Tim, go tell his wife. And tell her she'll have to come down and make final identification for us."

"Me?" I said. "Why don't you send McKee? He's not the sensitive type. Or why don't you go? This whole cute little bit was your idea, anyhow, Lieutenant, remember?"

"Are you disobeying an order?"

Then I thought of something. "No," I told him. "It's all right. I'll go."

I left them and went to the house where Bogen's wife and kids lived. When she opened the door, I could see past her into the cheaply, plainly-furnished living room that somehow didn't look that way now, in the glow from the decorated tree. I could see the presents placed neatly around the tree. And peering around a corner of a bedroom, I saw the eyes, big with awe, of a little girl about six and a boy about two years older.

Mrs Bogen saw me standing there and looked a little frightened. "Yes?" she said. "What is it?"

I thought about the newspapers, then. I thought: "What's the use? It'll be in the newspapers tomorrow, anyhow." Then I remembered that it would be Christmas day; there wouldn't *be* any newspapers published tomorrow, and few people would bother about turning on radios or television sets.

"Don't be alarmed," I told her, then. "I'm just letting the people in the neighborhood know what happened. We surprised a burglar at work, ma'am, and he ran down this street. We caught up with him here and had to shoot him. But it's all over now. We don't want anyone coming out, creating any more disturbance, so just go back to bed, will you please?"

Her mouth and eyes opened very wide. "Who – who was it?" she said in a small, hollow voice.

"Nobody important," I said. "Some young hood."

"Oh," she said then and I could see the relief come over her face and I knew then that my hunch had been right and Bogen hadn't let her know he was coming; he'd wanted to surprise her. Otherwise she would have put two and two together.

I told her goodnight and turned away and heard her shut the door softly behind me.

When I went back to Mortell I said: "Poor Bogen. He walked into the trap for nothing. His folks aren't even home. I asked one of the neighbors and she said they'd gone to Mrs Bogen's mother's and wouldn't be back until the day after Christmas."

"Well, I'll be damned," Mortell said, watching the men from the morgue wagon loading Bogen onto a basket.

"Yes," I said. I wondered what Mortell would do to me when he learned what I'd done and he undoubtedly would, eventually. Right then I didn't much care. The big thing was that Mrs Bogen and those kids were going to have their Christmas as scheduled. Even when I came back and told her what had happened, the day after tomorrow, it wouldn't take away the other.

Maybe it wasn't very much that I'd given them but it was something and I felt a little better. Not much, but a little.

Biographical Notes

Robert Turner was born in New York City in 1915. He left school at 14 and joined the messenger service at New York University. He soon became a supervisor, and stayed at this job for ten years in all. He began writing crime stories for popular magazines and then worked as an editor for such a magazine. He became quite successful in this field: among other things, he founded a literary agency in New York, and was elected regional vice-president of the professional organization Mystery Writers of America.

Over the years he published a number of books (fiction and non-fiction) under various pseudonyms – for example, he wrote a series of three books on the activities of the Mafia under the pseudonym 'Don Romano'. He also wrote the scripts for several very popular television series (e.g. "Johnny Midnight", "Tombstone Territory"). Some of his stories have also been adapted for television. He now lives in Hollywood.

Annotations

46 1 **sixty-eight degrees** 68° Fahrenheit = 20° C – 2 **shrubbery** [ʌ] low bushes – 4 **wreath** circular arrangement of leaves; *here:* an American Christmas decoration – 10 **tender** friendly, loving, sympathetic – 11 **cop** *Am. sl.* policeman – **to pull duty** *sl.* to be on duty; to have to work – 13 **to grab** to catch – **con** *sl.* convict, prisoner – 14 **lifer** *sl.* person who has been sent to prison for life – 16 **Third-Grade** *Am.* policeman's rank – **beat** area guarded by policeman on foot (work done only by the lowest grade of policemen) – 21 **sedan** [sə'dæn] *Am.* car for four or more passengers – 22 **lieutenant** [lu:'tenənt] *Am.* high-ranking police officer – 24 **in charge** responsible (for s.th.) – **plumpish** [ʌ] rather plump (fat) –26 **precinct car** ['pri:sɪŋkt] *Am.* patrol car used to control a certain district of a town – 31 **to shift** to change (position) – 32 **What a deal!** What bad luck! How awful!

47 5 **Sarge** [sɑ:dʒ] *sl.* sergeant – 6 **to be nuts** *sl.* to be mad, crazy – 17 **to hound** to persecute, to be mean to – **stoolie** *Am. sl.* police informer (Spitzel); (also verb: 'to stool') – 19 **in my book** *coll.* as far as I am concerned; to me – 20 **if it broke me** even if it ruined me – 26 **to stick up** *sl.* to rob by threatening with a gun – **hit** *sl.* crime – 30 **a break** *coll.* a fair chance – 31 **wouldn't have any part of** would not have anything to do with – 38 **to go for a piece** *sl.* to reach for a gun

48 2 **skip it** *coll.* forget about it – 3 **doubted** did not think – **cab** *Am.* taxi – 4 **dough** [dəʊ] *Am. sl.* money – 7 **sigh** [saɪ] sound expressing disappointment, sadness or relief – 8 **to be relieved** *here:* to be let off duty by the arrival of the next patrol – 11 **to postpone** to put off – 16 **edge** *here:* sharp sound – 27 **groin** Leistengegend – 30 **sane** mentally healthy – **insensitive** [-'---] not having any feelings – 35 **to wind up** to end up – **burden** heavy load – 38 **phony** *coll.* not true; insincere – 39 **to stick** *coll.* to endure, to tolerate, to hold out – **to make up for** to compensate for

49 3 **at close range** from a short distance – 14 **string** *here:* line – 15 **pine** evergreen tree – 17 **to shove** [ʌ] *coll.* to push – 18 **cuffs** *here:* handcuffs, i.e. joined metal rings for fastening a person's hands – 19 **to cover** *here:* to stand with a gun in order to protect s.o. – 28 **slacks** loose-fitting trousers – 30 **gaudy** bright and showy – **foil** thin, metallic paper – **crew-cut** cut very close to the scalp – 32 **disguise** [dɪs'gaɪz] costume or mask hiding one's real appearance – 33 **stride** long step – 35 **bull-froggy** loud and unpleasant – 40 **to whirr** [wɜː] to move with a buzzing sound

50 3 **a bride** woman getting married – 4 **liquid** ['lɪkwɪd] substance which can flow like water – **to trickle** to flow in drops or in a thin stream – **to figure** ['fɪgə] to guess, to come to the conclusion – 7 **to spin around** to turn round fast – 8 **to squeeze the trigger** to fire a gun – 12 **to jolt** [əʊ] to knock sharply – **heel** *here:* back part – **to stagger** to move unsteadily – 13 **to twist** to turn – 14 **flash** *here:* flashlight, torch – 16 **to resist** *here:* to stop oneself – 29 **cute** *Am. coll.* pleasant, attractive – 35 **glow** soft light – 36 **neat** tidy – 37 **to peer** to look very carefully – 38 **awe** [ɔː] feeling of respect mixed with fear

51 4 **to bother about** to be interested in, to take the trouble to do s.th. – 6 **burglar** thief who breaks into houses – 7 **ma'am** [mæm] short for 'Madam' (respectful form of address) – 11 **hollow** *here:* with a quality of emptiness – 12 **hood** [hʊd] *Am. sl.* criminal – 14 **hunch** *coll.* suspicion, intuitive idea – 15 **to put two and two together** *coll.* to draw an obvious conclusion – 23 **morgue wagon** [mɔːg] *Am.* car in which dead bodies are transported – 26 **eventually** at last, in the end – 28 **scheduled** ['ʃedjuːld] planned

Angelica Gibbs

The Test

On the afternoon Marian took her second driver's test, Mrs Ericson went with her. "It's probably better to have someone a little older with you," Mrs Ericson said as Marian slipped into the driver's seat beside her. "Perhaps the last time your Cousin Bill made you nervous, talking too much on the way."

"Yes, Ma'am," Marian said in her soft unaccented voice. "They probably do like it better if a white person shows up with you."

"Oh, I don't think it's *that,*" Mrs Ericson began, and subsided after a glance at the girl's set profile. Marian drove the car slowly through the shady suburban streets. It was one of the first hot days in June, and when they reached the boulevard they found it crowded with cars headed for the beaches.

"Do you want me to drive?" Mrs Ericson asked. "I'll be glad to if you're feeling jumpy." Marian shook her head. Mrs Ericson watched her dark, competent hands and wondered for the thousandth time how the house had ever managed to get along without her, or how she had lived through those earlier years when her household had been presided over by a series of slatternly white girls who had considered housework demeaning and the care of children an added insult. "You drive beautifully, Marian," she said. "Now, don't think of the last time. Anybody would slide on a steep hill on a wet day like that."

"It takes four mistakes to flunk you," Marian said. "I don't remember doing all the things the inspector marked down on my blank."

"People say that they only want you to slip them a little something," Mrs Ericson said doubtfully.

"No," Marian said. "That would only make it worse, Mrs Ericson, I know."

The car turned right, at a traffic signal, into a side road and slid up to the curb at the rear of a short line of parked cars. The inspectors had not arrived yet.

"You have the papers?" Mrs Ericson asked. Marian took them out of her bag: her learner's permit, the car registration, and her birth certificate. They settled down to the dreary business of waiting.

"It will be marvellous to have someone dependable to drive the children to school every day," Mrs Ericson said.

Marian looked up from the list of driving requirements she had been studying. "It'll make things simpler at the house, won't it?" she said.

"Oh Marian," Mrs Ericson exclaimed, "if I could only pay you half of what you're worth!"

"Now, Mrs Ericson," Marian said firmly. They looked at each other and smiled with affection.

Two cars with official insignia on their doors stopped across the street. The inspectors leaped out, very brisk and military in their neat uniforms. Marian's hands tightened on the wheel. "There's the one who flunked me last time," she whispered, pointing to a stocky, self-important man who had begun to shout directions at the driver at the head of the line. "Oh, Mrs Ericson."

"Now, Marian," Mrs Ericson said. They smiled at each other again, rather weakly.

The inspector who finally reached their car was not the stocky one but a genial, middle-aged man who grinned broadly as he thumbed over their papers Mrs Ericson started to get out of the car. "Don't you want to come along?" the inspector asked. "Mandy and I don't mind company."

Mrs Ericson was bewildered for a moment. "No," she said, and stepped to the curb. "I might make Marian self-conscious. She's a fine driver, Inspector."

"Sure thing," the inspector said, winking at Mrs Ericson. He slid into the seat beside Marian. "Turn right at the corner, Mandy-Lou."

From the curb, Mrs Ericson watched the car move smoothly up the street.

The inspector made notations in a small black book. "Age?" he inquired presently, as they drove along.

"Twenty-seven."

He looked at Marian out of the corner of his eye. "Old enough to have quite a flock of pickaninnies, eh?"

Marian did not answer.

"Left at this corner," the inspector said, "and park between that truck and the green Buick."

The two cars were very close together, but Marian squeezed in between them without too much maneuvering. "Driven before, Mandy-Lou?" the inspector asked.

"Yes, sir. I had a license for three years in Pennsylvania."

"Why do you want to drive a car?"

"My employer needs me to take her children to and from school."

"Sure you don't really want to sneak out nights to meet some young blood?" the inspector asked. He laughed as Marian shook her head.

"Let's see you take a left at the corner and then turn around in the middle of the next block," the inspector said. He began to whistle "Swanee River." "Make you homesick?" he asked.

Marian put out her hand, swung around neatly in the street, and headed back in the direction from which they had come. "No," she said. "I was born in Scranton, Pennsylvania."

The inspector feigned astonishment. "You-all ain't Southern?" he said. "Well, dog my cats if I didn't think you-all came from down yondah."

"No, sir," Marian said.

"Turn onto Main Street and let's see how you-all does in heavier traffic."

They followed a line of cars along Main Street for several blocks until they came in sight of a concrete bridge which arched high over the railroad tracks.

"Read that sign at the end of the bridge," the inspector said.

"'Proceed with caution. Dangerous in slippery weather,'" Marian said.

"You-all sho can read fine," the inspector exclaimed. "Where d'you learn to do that, Mandy?"

"I got my college degree last year," Marian said. Her voice was not quite steady.

As the car crept up the slope of the bridge the inspector burst out laughing. He laughed so hard he could scarcely give his next direction. "Stop here," he said, wiping his eyes, "then start 'er up again. Mandy got her degree, did she? Dog my cats!"

Marian pulled up beside the curb. She put the car in neutral, pulled on the emergency, waited a moment, and then put the car into gear again. Her face was set. As she released the brake her foot slipped off the clutch pedal and the engine stalled.

"Now, Mistress Mandy," the inspector said, "remember your degree."

"*Damn* you!" Marian cried. She started the car with a jerk.

The inspector lost his joviality in an instant. "Return to the starting place, please," he said, and made four very black crosses at random in the squares on Marian's application blank.

Mrs Ericson was waiting at the curb where they had left her. As Marian stopped the car, the inspector jumped out and brushed past her, his face purple. "What happened?" Mrs Ericson asked, looked after him with alarm.

Marian stared down at the wheel and her lip trembled.

"Oh, Marian, *again*?" Mrs Ericson said.

Marian nodded. "In a sort of different way," she said, and slid over to the right-hand side of the car.

Biographical Notes

"The Test" was first published in The New Yorker *in 1940. Although the story was widely anthologized in the U.S.A. and Britain, no information can be obtained on the author, nor are any other works by her known to the editors of this collection.*

Annotations

54 6 **Ma'am** [mæm] short for 'Madam' (respectful form of address) – **unaccented** without emphasis; in a neutral accent – 7 **to show up** *coll.* to come, to arrive – 8 **to subside** *here:* to become quiet; to stop talking – 9 **set** *here:* with a fixed expression – 11 **to head for** to move towards, to go in the direction of – 14 **jumpy** excited and nervous – 15 **competent** ['– – –] able, skilled – 17 **to preside over** to control, to be in charge of – 18 **slatternly** (of women) dirty, careless and untidy – **demeaning** lowering in status, beneath one's dignity – 19 **insult** ['– –] offence to one's pride – 20 **to slide** to slip on a smooth surface; to skid – 22 **to flunk s.o.** *Am. coll.* to fail s.o. in an exam or test – 23 **blank** form to be filled in – 24 **to slip them ... something** to give them some money secretly – 25 **doubtful** ['daʊtfəl] uncertain – 29 **curb** *Am.* (= *Br.* kerb) edge of footpath – 32 **certificate** [–'ɪ – –] official document – 33 **dreary** dull, boring

55 1 **marvellous** ['– – –] wonderful – **dependable** [–'– – –] that can be trusted – 3 **requirement** s.th. demanded – 7 **firm** strong and sure – 8 **affection** liking – 9 **insignia** [ɪn'sɪgnɪə] emblems – 10 **brisk** quick, active – **neat** tidy – 11 **to tighten** *here:* to hold more firmly – 12 **stocky** short, thick-set – 13 **directions** *here:* instructions – 18 **genial** ['dʒiːnɪəl] friendly, sympathetic – **to thumb over** *here:* to look through quickly, leafing through with one's thumb – 21 **bewildered** [bɪ'wɪldəd] confused – 22 **self-conscious** nervous and uncomfortable about oneself – 24 **to wink** to close and open one eye quickly – 26 **smoothly** without sudden changes or breaks – 31 **flock** large number (usually of birds or animals) – **pickaninny** (patronizing or derogatory term) Negro child – 34 **Buick** ['bjʊɪk] make of car – 35 **to squeeze in** to force oneself into a small space – 38 **Pennsylvania** U.S. State between Maryland and New York

56 1 **to sneak** to go quietly and secretly – **young blood** *old sl.* handsome young man – 4 **Swanee River** reference to a popular American song about Negroes in the South (first line: "Way down upon de Swanee River, far far away ...") – 9 **to feign** [feɪn] to make a false show of – **astonishment** [–'– – –] great surprise – **you-all** Southern dialect plural form of 'you' (Note that the inspector wrongly uses it as a singular.) – **Southern** from the Southern States, i.e. the former slave-holding States of the U.S. – 10 **dog my cats** *sl.* exclamation of surprise, another attempt to imitate Southern dialect – **yondah = yonder** there (The spelling indicates an attempt to imitate Southern or Black pronunciation, which in this case is similar to British Standard.) – 12 **you-all does** (The 'ungrammatical' verb form is typical of Black English.) – 14 **to arch** to make an upward curve – 17 **to proceed** to move forward – **caution** great care – 18 **sho** = sure (See note on 'yondah' above.) – 20 **college degree** academic title acquired after passing an exam – 21 **steady** sure and even (in tone) – 22 **to creep (crept, crept)** to move slowly – **slope** rising or falling ground – 26 **to pull up** to come to a stop, to stop – **neutral** Leerlauf – **to pull on** to draw one end of s.th. with force – 27 **emergency** *here:* handbrake – **gear** one of the four speeds of a car – 28 **to release** to set free, to unfasten – **clutch** pedal pressed with one's left foot when changing gears – 29 **to stall** [ɔ:] to stop suddenly – 32 **joviality** [ˌdʒəʊvɪ'ælɪtɪ] joking manner – **in an instant** at once – 33 **at random** without system – 36 **to brush past** to just touch s.o. as one quickly passes – 37 **purple** dark reddish-blue – 38 **alarm** fear, a feeling of impending disaster – 39 **to tremble** to shake

Dal Stivens

The Pepper-Tree

My father often spoke about the pepper-tree when we were kids, and it was clear it meant a lot to him. It stood for something – like the Rolls-Royce he was always going to buy. It wasn't what he said about the pepper-tree – my father had no great gift for words – but how he said it that counted. When he spoke of the pepper-tree at Tullama where he had been brought up you saw it clearly; a monster of a tree with long shawls of olive-green leaves in a big generous country-town backyard. "A decent backyard – none of your city pocket-handkerchief lots," my father said. There were berries on the tree that turned from green to pink with waxlike covers which you could unpick and get the sticky smell of them all over your fingers. In this spanking tree there was always, too, a noisy traffic of sparrows and starlings fluttering and hopping from branch to branch.

When we lived at Newtown, Sydney, I used to look for pepper-trees when my father took me for a walk on Sunday afternoons. "Look, there's a pepper-tree," I'd say to him when I saw one with its herring-bone leaves.

"By golly, boy, that's only a little runt of a tree," my old man would say. "They don't do so well in the city. Too much smoke, by golly. You ought to see them out west where I come from."

My father was a tall, thin man with melancholy brown eyes and the soul of a poet. It was the poet in him that wanted to own a Rolls-Royce one day.

"First our own house and then some day, when my ship comes home, I'll buy a Rolls-Royce," he'd say.

Some of his friends thought my old man was a little crazy to have such an ambition.

"What would you do with one of those flash cars, Peter?" they'd tease him. "Go and live among the swells?"

My father would stroke his long brown moustache, which had only a few bits of white in it, and try to explain, but he couldn't make them understand. He couldn't even get his ideas across to my mother. Only now do I think I understand what a Rolls-Royce meant to him.

"I don't want to swank it, as you put it, Emily," he'd say to my mother. "No, by golly. I want to own a Rolls-Royce because it is the most perfect piece of machinery made in this world. Why, a Rolls-Royce –"

And then he'd stop and you could feel him groping for the right words to describe what he felt, and then go on blunderingly with the caress of a lover in his voice, talking about how beautiful the engine was. . . .

"What would a garage mechanic do with a Rolls-Royce, I ask you!" my mother would say. "I'd feel silly sitting up in it."

At such times my mother would give the wood stove in the kitchen a good shove with the poker, or swish her broom vigorously. My mother was a small plump woman with brown hair which she wore drawn tight back from her forehead.

Like the pepper-tree, the Rolls-Royce symbolized something for my father. He had been born in Tullama in the mallee. His father was a bricklayer and wanted his son to follow him. But my father had had his mind set on becoming an engineer. When he was eighteen he had left Tullama and come to the city and got himself apprenticed to a mechanical engineer. He went to technical classes in the evening. After two years his eyes had given out on him.

"If I had had some money things might have been different, by golly," my father told me once. "I could have gone to the university and learnt things properly. I could have become a civil engineer. I didn't give my eyes a fair go – I went to classes five nights a week and studied after I came home."

After his eyes went, my father had to take unskilled jobs but always near machinery. "I like tinkering but I had no proper schooling," he said once.

He knew a lot and in spite of his eyes he could only have learnt most of it from books. He knew all about rocks and how they were formed. He could talk for hours, if you got him started, about fossils and the story of evolution. My mother didn't like to hear him talking about such things because she thought such talk was irreligious. Looking back now I'd say that in spite of his lack of orthodox schooling my father was a learned man. He taught me more than all the teachers I ever had at high school. He was a keen naturalist, too.

Just before the depression came when we were living at Newtown, my father had paid one hundred pounds off the house. He was forty-seven years old then. I was twelve.

"By golly, we'll own the house before we know where we are," he said.

"Will we?" said my mother. "At a pound a week we have twelve years to go – unless we win Tatts."

"You never know what may turn up," said my old man cheerfully.

"I have a good idea what with people losing their jobs every day."

"I haven't lost mine," my father said, "and what's more, if I do, I have a way of making some money."

"I suppose it's another of your inventions, Peter? What is it this time, I ask you?"

"Never you mind," said my father. But he said it gently.

One of my mother's complaints was that my father was always losing money on the things he tried to invent. Another was that he was always filling the backyard up with junk.

"What can you do with these pocket-handkerchief lots?" my father would say. "Now, when I was a nipper at Tullama we had a decent backyard – why it was immense – it was as big –"

He'd stop there not being able to get the right word.

Auction sales, according to my mother, were one of my father's weaknesses. He could never resist anything if it looked cheap, even if he had no use for it, she'd say. Soon after my old man had told my mother he had something in mind to make some money, he went away early one Sunday morning. He came back about lunch-time in a motor lorry. On the back of the Ford was a two-stroke kerosene engine. I came running out.

"I've bought it, Joe, by golly," he told me.

He had, too. Both engine and lorry.

"Dirt cheap. Forty quid the lot," he said. "Ten quid down, boy, and ten bob a week."

My mother cut up when she heard.

"Wasting money when it could have gone into the house, Peter."

"This'll pay the house off in no time, by golly," my father said. "And buy a lot of other things, too."

I knew by the way he looked up and over my mother's head he was thinking of the Rolls-Royce which to him was like a fine poem or a great symphony of Beethoven.

All that day he was very excited, walking round the engine, standing back to admire it, and then peering closely at it. He started it running and stopped it continually all the afternoon. Every night when he came home from the garage during the next week, he'd go first thing and look at the engine. He had some plan in his mind but wouldn't say what it was at first.

"Wait and see, Joe," he'd said. "You'll see all right."

He didn't let me into his secret for over a week, although I knew he was bursting to tell someone. In the end, he drew me aside mysteriously in the kitchen one night, when my mother was in the bedroom, and whispered, "It's an invention for cleaning out underground wells, boy."

"For cleaning out wells?"

"Underground wells."

He listened to hear if my mother was coming back.

"I'm rigging a light out there tonight, boy," he whispered. "Come out later and I'll show you."

My father's idea, he explained later, was to clean underground wells in country towns by suction. You pushed a stiff brush on the end of the pipe down the sides and along the bottom of underground wells. The pipe sucked up the silt and you didn't lose much water from the well.

"Every country town has half a dozen underground wells, boy," he said. "The banks and one or two of the wealthier blokes in the town. Just like it was in Tullama. There's money in it because you can clean the well out without losing too much water. It's a gold-mine."

It sounded good to me.

"When do you start?" I asked.

"Soon, by golly," he said. "The job at the garage won't spin out much longer."

He was right about that, but until the day she died my mother always had a sneaking idea that the old man had helped to give himself the sack. It was early in 1930 when the old man set out in the lorry, heading out west.

"You've got to go to the low-rainfall districts," he said.

"Like Tullama?" I said.

"Yes, like Tullama, by golly."

I started thinking of the pepper-tree then.

"Will you go to Tullama and see the pepper-tree?"

My father stroked his long straggling moustache. Into his eyes came that look like when he was thinking or talking about the Rolls. He didn't answer me for a bit.

"By golly, yes, boy, if I go there."

Soon after this he started off. Every week brought a letter from him. He did well too. He was heading almost due west from Sydney and I followed the towns he spoke of in my school atlas. It took him nearly a day on a well, so in the larger towns he might stay over a week, in the smaller a day or a day and a half.

After he had been away for two months he still had a good few wells to go before he reached Tullama. You could see that he was heading that way.

"Him and that silly pepper-tree!" said my mother, but she didn't say it angrily. My father was sending her as much money as he used to bring home when he worked at the garage.

But in spite of what my mother said about the pepper-tree, she became a bit keen as my father got only two weeks off Tullama. She made a small pin-flag for me to stick on the map. About this time a change came in the old man's letters home. At first they had been elated, but now they were quieter He didn't boast so much about the money he was making, or say anything about the Rolls. Perhaps excitement was making him quieter as he got nearer to the pepper-tree, I thought.

"I know what it is," my mother said. "He's not getting his proper meals. He's too old to be gallivanting off on his own. I bet he's not cooking proper meals for himself. And without a decent bed to sleep in – only the back of that lorry."

I thought the day would never come, but soon enough my dad had only one town to do before he would reach Tullama. His letters usually arrived on a Tuesday – he wrote home on the Sundays – but round this time I watched for the mail every day and was late for school three mornings running. When a letter did come I grabbed it from the postman's hand and hurried inside with it, reading the post-mark on the run. It was from Tullama.

"All right, all right, don't rush me, Joe," my mother said. "You and your pepper-tree."

I read over her elbow. There was only one page. There was nothing about the pepper-tree. Dad was well and making money, but he was thinking of returning soon. Only a few lines.

I couldn't understand it.

On the next Tuesday there was no letter. Nor on the Wednesday. On the Thursday my father came home. He turned up at breakfast-time. He gave us a surprise walking in like that. He said that he had sold the truck and engine and come home by train. He looked tired and shamefaced and somehow a lot older. I saw a lot more white in his moustache.

"The engine was no good," he said. "It kept breaking down. It cost me nearly all I earned and it was hungry on petrol. I had to sell it to pay back what I borrowed and get my fare home."

"Oh Peter," my mother said, putting her arms round him. "You poor darling. I knew something was wrong."

"Mother reckoned it was the food," I said. "She reckoned you weren't getting your proper meals."

"I'll make you a cup of tea, Peter," my mother said, bustling over to the stove and pushing another piece of wood into it. "Then I'll get you some breakfast."

"By golly, that sounds a bit of all right," my father said then. This was the first time since he had walked in that he had sounded like his old self.

My mother hurried about the kitchen and my father talked a bit more. "I thought I was going to do well at first," he said. "But the engine was too old. It was always spare parts. It ate up all I earned."

He talked on about the trip. I had got over my surprise at seeing him walk in and now wanted to know all about the pepper-tree.

"Did you see the pepper-tree, dad?"

"Yes, I saw it all right."

I stood directly in front of him as he sat at the table, but he was not looking at me but at something far away. He didn't answer for what seemed a long time.

"It was a little runt of a tree, boy – and a little backyard."

He wouldn't say any more than that and he never spoke of the pepper-tree – or the Rolls – again.

Biographical Notes

Dallas George Stivens, a fifth-generation Australian, was born in New South Wales in 1911 and was educated in Sydney. During World War II he joined the Australian Army Education Service and afterwards worked in the Australian Department of Information.

Dal Stivens is best known for his satirical novel Jimmy Brockett, *which was first published in 1951. A number of other novels, and several collections of short stories followed in the fifties and sixties. Dal Stivens was a recipient of the Commonwealth Literary Fund Fellowship in 1951, 1962 and 1970. Commenting on his own work, he says his "underlying interest has been in the tension between illusion and reality, art and life". This is something which comes out clearly in our story. Dal Stivens is married and has two children.*

Annotations

59 **pepper-tree** subtropical evergreen tree with bright red fruit – 4 **gift** *here:* talent – 5 **Tullama** probably Tullamore, a small town in New South Wales – 7 **generous** *here:* with lots of space – **decent** ['di:sənt] *coll.* proper, as it should be; of the right size – 8 **lot** area of land (Parzelle) – 10 **to unpick** to take out from – **spanking** *coll.* fine, excellent – 11 **sparrow** common small brownish bird (Sperling) – **starling** common greenish-black bird (Star) – 12 **to flutter** (of birds) to move the wings quickly – 16 **by golly** *Austr. sl.* expression of surprise (= by God) – **runt** an underdeveloped specimen – 17 **don't do so well** don't grow so well – 19 **melancholy** ['– – – –] sad – 24 **ambition** strong desire (for success, etc.) – 25 **flash** *coll.* costly-looking – **to tease** to make fun of – 26 **the swells** *sl.* rich and elegant people – 27 **to stroke** to rub gently – 29 **to get s.th. across** *coll.* to make o.s. understood – 31 **to swank it** *coll.* to show off – **as you put it** as you say

60 1 **to grope for** to search for uncertainly – 2 **to blunder** *here:* to express one's thoughts or feelings in an awkward manner – **caress** [kə'res] gesture expressing love – 7 **shove** [ʃʌv] heavy push – **poker** long metal stick for stirring a fire – **to swish** to move s.th. (through the air) with a sharp whistling sound – **broom** long-handled sweeping brush (Besen) – **vigorous** ['vɪgərəs] strong – 9 **forehead** ['fɒrɪd] part of the face above the eyes – 11 **in the mallee** ['mæli:] in the bush; out in the eucalyptus forests – **bricklayer** person who builds walls and houses with bricks – 12 **to set one's mind on** to want very much – 14 **to get o.s. apprenticed to s.o.** to start training in a particular skill – 15 **to give out** *coll.* to lose, to break down – 19 **civil engineer** engineer responsible for planning, building and repairing public works (Bauingenieur) – **a fair go** a fair chance – 21 **after his eyes went** after his eyesight became bad – **unskilled jobs** jobs for untrained workers – 22 **to tinker** to play around with (machines) – 28 **orthodox** proper, conventional – **learned** ['lɜːnɪd] having very much knowledge – 24 **keen** very interested, enthusiastic – 30 **naturalist** person who studies plants and animals – 31 **depression** economic crisis with high unemployment – 32 **to pay ... off the house** to pay back some of the debt on the house – 36 **Tatts** an Australian lottery – 38 **what with** considering

61 3 **never you mind** that's none of your business – 6 **junk** *coll.* old things of little or no value – 8 **nipper** *Austr. coll.* small child – 12 **to resist s.th.** *here:* to keep away from – 16 **two-stroke engine** Zweitaktmotor – **kerosene** oil distilled from petroleum – 19 **dirt cheap** *coll.* very cheap – **quid** *sl.* a pound (£ 1); *here:* Australian pound (nowadays, the monetary unit of Australia is the dollar) – **the lot** number of articles sold (or bought) together – **ten quid down** £ 10 in cash – 20 **bob** *coll.* shilling (now 5p) – 21 **to cut up** *coll.* to be very upset or angry – 29 **to admire** *here:* to look at with pleasure – **to peer** to look carefully – 30 **continually** over and over again – 35 **bursting to do s.th.** wanting very much to do s.th.; waiting for an opportunity – 37 **well** hole drilled into the earth to get water

62 1 **to rig s.th.** to construct, to put up – 4 **suction** act of sucking (Saugwirkung) – **stiff** not easily movable; not flexible – 6 **silt** loose sand, mud – 8 **bloke** *sl.* fellow, man – 13 **to spin out** *here:* to last, to continue – 16 **sneaking** vague, not clearly or openly expressed – **to give s.o. the sack** to dismiss (from a job), to fire – 23 **straggling** spread untidily – 28 **to head** to move in a certain direction – **due west** directly west – 40 **elated** filled with pride and joy

63 1 **to boast** to talk proudly – 5 **to gallivant** [ˌ– –ˈ–] *coll.* to travel around, to go off amusing o.s. – **on one's own** alone – 11 **three mornings running** ... one after another, in a row – 12 **to grab** to snatch, to take in one's hand quickly – 13 **on the run** *here:* while hurrying – 22 **to turn up** to arrive – 24 **shamefaced** looking as if one is ashamed of s.th. – 33 **to bustle** ['bʌsl] to appear to be very busy – 36 **a bit of all right** *sl.* fine, great – 40 **spare parts** Ersatzteile – **it was always ...** *here:* it always needed ... – **to eat up** *here:* to use up

William Saroyan

The Great Leapfrog Contest

Rosie Mahoney was a tough little Irish kid whose folks, through some miscalculation in directions, or out of an innate spirit of anarchy, had moved into the Russian-Italian-and-Greek neighborhood of my home town, across the Southern Pacific tracks, around G Street.

She wore a turtle-neck sweater, usually red. Her father was a bricklayer named Cull and a heavy drinker. Her mother's name was Mary. Mary Mahoney used to go to the Greek Orthodox Catholic Church on Kearny Boulevard every Sunday, because there was no Irish Church to go to anywhere in the neighborhood. The family seemed to be a happy one.

Rosie's three brothers had all grown up and gone to sea. Her two sisters had married. Rosie was the last of the clan. She had entered the world when her father had been close to sixty and her mother in her early fifties. For all that, she was hardly the studious or scholarly type.

Rosie had little use for girls, and as far as possible avoided them. She had less use for boys, but found it undesirable to avoid them. That is to say, she made it a point to take part in everything the boys did. She was always on hand, and always the first to take up any daring or crazy idea. Everybody felt awkward about her continuous presence, but it was no use trying to chase her away, because that meant a fight in which she asked no quarter, and gave none.

If she didn't whip every boy she fought, every fight was at least an honest draw, with a slight edge in Rosie's favor. She didn't fight girl-style, or cry if hurt. She fought the regular style and took advantage of every opening. It was very humiliating to be hurt by Rosie, so after a while any boy who thought of trying to chase her away, decided not to.

It was no use. She just wouldn't go. She didn't seem to like any of the boys especially, but she liked being in on any mischief they might have in mind, and she wanted to play on any teams they organized. She was an excellent baseball player, being as good as anybody else in the neighborhood at any position, and for her age an expert pitcher. She had a wicked wing, too, and could throw a ball in from left field that when it hit the catcher's mitt it made a nice sound.

She was extraordinarily swift on her feet and played a beautiful game of tin-can hockey.

At pee-wee, she seemed to have the most disgusting luck in the world.

At the game we invented and used to call *Horse* she was as good at *horse* as at *rider,* and she insisted on following the rules of the game. She insisted on being horse when it was her turn to be horse. This always embarrassed her partner, whoever he happened to be, because it didn't seem right for a boy to be getting up on the back of a girl.

She was an excellent football player too.

As a matter of fact, she was just naturally the equal of any boy in the neighborhood, and much the superior of many of them. Especially after she had lived in the neighborhood three years. It took her that long to make everybody understand that she had come to stay and that she was *going* to stay.

She did, too; even after the arrival of a boy named Rex Folger, who was from somewhere in the south of Texas. This boy Rex was a natural-born leader. Two months after his arrival in the neighborhood, it was understood by everyone that if Rex wasn't the leader of the gang, he was very nearly the leader. He had fought and licked every boy in the neighborhood who at one time or another had fancied himself leader. And he had done so without any noticeable ill-feeling, pride, or ambition.

As a matter of fact, no one could possibly have been more good-natured than Rex. Everybody resented him, just the same.

One winter, the whole neighborhood took to playing a game that had become popular on the other side of the tracks, in another slum neighborhood of the town: *Leapfrog.* The idea was for as many boys as cared to participate, to bend down and be leaped over by every other boy in the game, and then himself to get up and begin leaping over all the other boys, and then bend down again until all the boys had leaped over him again, and keep this up until all the other players had become exhausted. This didn't happen, sometimes, until the last two players had traveled a distance of three our four miles, while the other players walked along, watching and making bets.

Rosie, of course, was always in on the game. She was always one of the last to drop out, too. And she was the only person in the neighborhood Rex Folger hadn't fought and beaten.

He felt that that was much too humiliating even to think about. But inasmuch as she seemed to be a member of the gang, he felt that in some way or another he ought to prove his superiority.

One summer day during vacation, an argument between Rex and Rosie developed and Rosie pulled off her turtle-neck sweater and challenged him to a fight. Rex took a cigarette from his pocket, lighted it, inhaled, and told Rosie he wasn't in the habit of hitting women – where he came from that amounted to boxing your mother. On the other hand, he said, if Rosie cared to compete with him in any other sport, he would be glad to oblige her. Rex was a very calm and courteous conversationalist. He had poise. It was unconscious, of course, but he had it just the same. He was just naturally a man who couldn't be hurried, flustered, or excited.

So Rex and Rosie fought it out in this game Leapfrog. They got to leaping over one another, quickly, too, until the first thing we knew the whole gang of us was out on the State Highway going south towards Fowler. It was a very hot day. Rosie and Rex were in great shape, and it looked like one was tougher than the other and more stubborn. They talked a good deal, especially Rosie, who insisted that she would have to fall down unconscious before she'd give up to a guy like Rex.

He said he was sorry his opponent was a girl. It grieved him deeply to have to make a girl exert herself to the point of death, but it was just too bad. He had to, so he had to. They leaped and squatted, leaped and squatted, and we got out to Sam Day's vineyard. That was half-way to Fowler. It didn't seem like either Rosie or Rex was ever going to get tired. They hadn't even begun to show signs of growing tired, although each of them was sweating a great deal.

Naturally, we were sure Rex would win the contest. But that was because we hadn't taken into account the fact that he was a simple person, whereas Rosie was crafty and shrewd. Rosie knew how to figure angles. She had discovered how to jump over Rex Folger in a way that weakened him. And after a while, about three miles out of Fowler, we noticed that she was coming down on Rex's *neck,* instead of on his back. Naturally, this was hurting him and making the blood rush to his head. Rosie herself squatted in such a way that it was impossible, almost, for Rex to get anywhere near her neck with his hands.

Before long, we noticed that Rex was weakening. His head was getting closer and closer to the ground. About a half mile out of Fowler, we heard Rex's head bumping the ground every time Rosie leaped over him. They were good loud bumps that we knew were painful, but Rex wasn't complaining. He was too proud to complain.

Rosie, on the other hand, knew she had her man, and she was giving him all she had. She was bumping his head on the ground as solidly as she could, because she knew she didn't have much more fight in her, and if she didn't lay him out cold, in the hot sun, in the next ten minutes or so, she would fall down exhausted herself, and lose the contest.

Suddenly Rosie bumped Rex's head a real powerful one. He got up very dazed and very angry. It was the first time we had ever seen him fuming. By God, the girl was taking advantage of him, if he wasn't mistaken, and he didn't like it. Rosie was squatted in front of him. He came up groggy and paused a moment. Then he gave Rosie a very effective kick that sent her sprawling. Rosie jumped up and smacked Rex in the mouth. The gang jumped in and tried to establish order.

It was agreed that the Leapfrog contest must not change into a fight. Not any more. Not with Fowler only five or ten minutes away. The gang ruled further that Rex had had no right to kick Rosie and that in smacking him in the mouth Rosie had squared the matter, and the contest was to continue.

Rosie was very tired and sore; and so was Rex. They began leaping and squatting again; and again we saw Rosie coming down on Rex's neck so that his head was bumping the ground.

It looked pretty bad for the boy from Texas. We couldn't understand how he could take so much punishment. We all felt that Rex was getting what he had coming to him, but at the same time everybody seemed to feel badly about Rosie, a girl, doing the job instead of one of us. Of course, that was where we were wrong. Nobody but Rosie could have figured out that smart way of humiliating a very powerful and superior boy. It was probably the woman in her, which, less than five years later, came out to such an extent that she became one of the most beautiful girls in town, gave up tomboy activities, and married one of the wealthiest young men in Kings County, a college man named, if memory serves, Wallace Hadington Finlay VI.

Less than a hundred yards from the heart of Fowler, Rosie, with great and admirable artistry, finished the job.

That was where the dirt of the highway siding ended and the paved main street of Fowler began. This street was paved with cement, not asphalt. Asphalt, in that heat, would have been too soft to serve, but cement had exactly the right degree of brittleness. I think Rex, when he squatted over the hard cement, knew the game was up. But he was brave to the end. He squatted over the hard cement and waited for the worst. Behind him, Rosie Mahoney prepared to make the supreme effort. In this next leap, she intended to give her all, which she did.

She came down on Rex Folger's neck like a ton of bricks. His head banged against the hard cement, his body straightened out, and his arms and legs twitched.

He was out like a light.

Six paces in front of him, Rosie Mahoney squatted and waited. Jim Telesco counted twenty, which was the time allowed for each leap. Rex didn't get up during the count.

The contest was over. The winner of the contest was Rosie Mahoney.

Rex didn't get up by himself at all. He just stayed where he was until a half-dozen of us lifted him and carried him to a horse trough, where we splashed water on his face.

Rex was a confused young man all the way back. He was also a deeply humiliated one. He couldn't understand anything about anything. He just looked dazed and speechless. Every now and then we imagined he wanted to talk, and I guess he did, but after we'd all gotten ready to hear what he had to say, he couldn't speak. He made a gesture so tragic that tears came to the eyes of eleven members of the gang.

Rosie Mahoney, on the other hand, talked all the way home. She said everything.

I think it made a better man of Rex. More human. After that he was a gentler sort of soul. It may have been because he couldn't see very well for some time. At any rate, for weeks he seemed to be going around in a dream. His gaze would freeze on some insignificant object far away in the landscape, and half the time it seemed as if he didn't know where he was going, or why. He took little part in the activities of the gang, and the following winter he stayed away altogether. He came to school one day wearing glasses. He looked broken and pathetic.

That winter Rosie Mahoney stopped hanging around with the gang, too. She had a flair for making an exit at the right time.

Biographical Notes

William Saroyan (1908–1981) was born in California of Armenian parents. His father had come to America because of political persecution in his home country. At an early age he made up his mind to become a writer and started reading extensively. He had to leave school at 15 to earn his living, and worked at a number of jobs.

His literary career began when his collection of short stories The Daring Young Man on the Flying Trapeze *was published in 1934. In the years to follow, he published several more. His play* The Time of Your Life *won the highly-regarded Pulitzer Prize in 1939, but he refused it because he was opposed to patronage of the arts by business. His best-known work is* The Human Comedy *(1943), a novel which has been translated into many languages; it was later made into a film.*

Many of Saroyan's stories are semi-autobiographical, or deal with the kind of immigrant community he grew up in. In all of his works, he expresses something of his great love for the ordinary people of America.

Annotations

67 **leapfrog** children's game in which one player bends down and another jumps over him/her – **contest** ['––] competition – 1 **folks** *coll.* family; relatives or parents – 2 **innate** [ɪ'neɪt] part of one's nature – 4 **Southern Pacific** one of the major American railway companies – **G Street** In some American towns streets don't have proper names but are identified by numbers or letters. – 5 **turtle-neck sweater** ['swetə] pullover with a high round collar – **bricklayer** person whose work is to build with bricks (Ziegelsteine) – 11 **clan** large family – 12 **for all that** in spite of this – 13 **studious, scholarly** fond of learning or studying – 15 **undesirable** not to be wished for – 16 **to make it a point to do s.th.** to make a special effort to do s.th. – 17 **daring** unusual, requiring courage – 18 **awkward** uncomfortable – 19 **to ask no quarter** not to expect pity – 21 **to whip** *here:* to beat, to defeat – **honest** *here:* fair – 22 **a draw** (of contests) undecided – **a slight edge** a little bit – 23 **opening** *here:* opportunity – 24 **to humiliate** [hju:'mɪlɪeɪt] to make s.o. feel ashamed – 27 **to be in on s.th.** to take part in s.th. – **mischief** ['mɪstʃɪf] foolish behaviour, trouble, trickery – 30 **pitcher (in baseball)** player who throws the ball – **had a wicked wing** *coll.* was very good in wing (far-side) position – 32 **catcher's mitt** strong hand-covering worn by a baseball player

68 1 **swift** quick – 3 **pee-wee** game of marbles (Murmeln) – **disgusting** *here:* annoying – 6 **to embarrass** to make (s.o.) feel uncomfortable – 10 **to be the equal of** to be as good as – 19 **to lick** *coll.* to beat, to defeat – 20 **to fancy o.s.** to imagine oneself to be – 21

ambition strong desire for success – 23 **to resent** [rɪ'zent] to feel angry at or unhappy about – 24 **to take to** to take up, to start doing – 26 **to care to** to like, to want – 30 **exhausted** very tired – 38 **inasmuch as** since, because – 40 **argument** ['ɑ:gjʊmənt] quarrel

69 1 **to challenge s.o.** to call s.o. to take part in a fight or a contest – 4 **to amount to** to be the same as – 6 **to oblige** [ə'blaɪdʒ] to do s.o. a favour – **courteous** ['kɜ:tɪəs] polite – **conversationalist** one who is good at talking – 7 **poise** [pɔɪz] quiet self-confidence, ability to deal with all social situations – **unconscious** *here:* not done on purpose – 8 **to fluster s.o.** to make s.o. nervous – 13 **in great shape** in good form, physically fit – 14 **stubborn** strong-willed – 17 **to grieve** [i:] to make (s.o.) very unhappy – 18 **to exert o.s.** [–'–] to put all one's energy into s.th. – 19 **to squat** [ɒ] to bend down – 20 **vineyard** ['vɪnjəd] piece of land used for wine production – 25 **to take into account** to consider – 26 **crafty, shrewd** [ʃru:d] clever and tricky – **to figure angles** *here:* to leap at the angle most advantageous to herself – 38 **she had her man** *coll.* she had gained the upper hand – 39 **solid** firm, strong

70 1 **to lay s.o. out cold** *coll.* to knock s.o. unconscious – 4 **dazed** dizzy, unable to think clearly – **to fume** to be very angry – 8 **to sprawl** to lie with one's arms and legs stretched out – **to smack** to hit – 13 **to square the matter** to make things equal – 14 **sore** with aching muscles – 18 **punishment** *here:* ill treatment – 19 **he had [it] coming to him** *coll.* he deserved it – 21 **to figure out** *coll.* to work out – **smart** *coll.* clever – 23 **to such an extent that** so much that – 24 **tomboy** girl who is fond of rough and noisy games – 28 **admirable** ['– – – –] excellent – 29 **siding** soft sand or earth along the side of a road – 32 **brittleness** hardness – 33 **the game was up** *coll.* the game was lost – 39 **to twitch** to make small, uncontrolled movements

71 1 **pace** step – 6 **trough** [trɒf] open box for animals to drink from – 18 **at any rate** in any case – 19 **gaze** long steady look – **insignificant** not important – 23 **pathetic** [pə'θetɪk] sad, pitiful – 25 **flair** instinct for effective behaviour

Katherine Mansfield

Her First Ball

Exactly when the ball began Leila would have found it hard to say. Perhaps her first real partner was the cab. It did not matter that she shared the cab with the Sheridan girls and their brother. She sat back in her own little corner of it, and the bolster on which her hand rested felt like the sleeve of an unknown young man's dress suit; and away they bowled, past waltzing lamp-posts and houses and fences and trees.

"Have you really never been to a ball before, Leila? But, my child, how too weird –" cried the Sheridan girls.

"Our nearest neighbour was fifteen miles," said Leila softly, gently opening and shutting her fan.

Oh dear, how hard it was to be indifferent like the others! She tried not to smile too much; she tried not to care. But every single thing was so new and exciting. Meg's tuberoses, Jose's long loop of amber, Laura's little dark head, pushing above her white fur like a flower through snow. She would remember for ever. It even gave her a pang to see her cousin Laurie throw away the wisps of tissue paper he pulled from the fastenings of his new gloves. She would like to have kept those wisps as a keepsake, as a remembrance. Laurie leaned forward and put his hand on Laura's knee.

"Look here, darling," he said. "The third and the ninth as usual. Twig?"

Oh, how marvellous to have a brother! In her excitement Leila felt that if there had been time, if it hadn't been impossible, she couldn't have helped crying because she was an only child and no brother had ever said "Twig?" to her; no sister would ever say, as Meg said to Jose that moment, "I've never known your hair go up more successfully than it has tonight."

But, of course, there was no time. They were at the drill hall already; there were cabs in front of them and cabs behind. The road was bright on either side with moving fanlike lights, and on the pavement gay couples seemed to float through the air; little satin shoes chased each other like birds.

"Hold on to me, Leila; you'll get lost," said Laura.

"Come on, girls, let's make a dash for it," said Laurie.

Leila put two fingers on Laura's pink velvet cloak, and they were somehow lifted past the big golden lantern, carried along the passage, and pushed into the little room marked 'Ladies'. Here the crowd was so great there was hardly space to take off their things; the noise was deafening. Two benches on either side were stacked high with wraps. Two old women in white aprons ran up and down tossing fresh armfuls. And everybody was pressing forward trying to get at the little dressing-table and mirror at the far end.

A great quivering jet of gas lighted the ladies' room. It couldn't wait; it was dancing already. When the door opened again and there came a burst of tuning from the drill hall, it leaped almost to the ceiling.

Dark girls, fair girls were patting their hair, tying ribbons again, tucking handkerchiefs down the fronts of their bodices, smoothing marble-white gloves. And because they were all laughing it seemed to Leila that they were all lovely.

"Aren't there any invisible hairpins?" cried a voice. "How most extraordinary! I can't see a single invisible hairpin."

"Powder my back, there's a darling," cried someone else.

"But I must have a needle and cotton. I've torn simply miles and miles of the frill," wailed a third.

Then, "Pass them along, pass them along!" The straw basket of programmes was tossed from arm to arm. Darling little pink-and-silver programmes, with pink pencils and fluffy tassels. Leila's fingers shook as she took one out of the basket. She wanted to ask someone, "Am I meant to have one too?" but she had just time to read: 'Waltz 3. *Two, Two in a Canoe*. Polka 4. *Making the Feathers Fly,'* when Meg cried, "Ready, Leila?" and they pressed their way through the crush in the passage towards the big double doors of the drill hall.

Dancing had not begun yet, but the band had stopped tuning, and the noise was so great it seemed that when it did begin to play it would never be heard. Leila, pressing close to Meg, looking over Meg's shoulder, felt that even the little quivering coloured flags strung across the ceiling were talking. She quite forgot to be shy; she forgot how in the middle of dressing she had sat down on the bed with one shoe off and one shoe on and begged her mother to ring up her cousins and say she couldn't go after all. And the rush of longing she had had to be sitting on the veranda of their forsaken up-country home, listening to the baby owls crying 'More pork' in the moonlight, was changed to a rush of joy so sweet that it was hard to bear alone. She clutched her fan, and, gazing at the gleaming, golden floor, the azaleas, the lanterns, the stage at one end with its red carpet and gilt chairs and the band in a corner, she thought breathlessly, 'How heavenly; how simply heavenly!'

All the girls stood grouped together at one side of the doors, the men at the other, and the chaperones in dark dresses, smiling rather foolishly, walked with little careful steps over the polished floor towards the stage.

"This is my little country cousin Leila. Be nice to her. Find her partners; she's under my wing," said Meg going up to one girl after another.

Strange faces smiled at Leila – sweetly, vaguely. Strange voices answered, "Of course, my dear." But Leila felt the girls didn't really see her. They were looking towards the men. Why didn't the men begin? What were they waiting for? There they stood, smoothing their gloves, patting their glossy hair and smiling among themselves. Then, quite suddenly, as if they had only just made up their minds that that was what they had to do, the men came gliding over the parquet. There was a joyful flutter among the girls. A tall, fair man flew up to Meg, seized her programme, scribbled something; Meg passed him on to Leila. "May I have the pleasure?" He ducked and smiled. There came a dark man wearing an eyeglass, then cousin Laurie came with a friend, and Laura with a little freckled fellow whose tie was crooked. Then quite an old man – fat, with a big bald patch on his head – took her programme and murmured, "Let me see, let me see!" And he was a long time comparing his programme, which looked black with names, with hers. It seemed to give him so much trouble that Leila was ashamed. "Oh, please don't bother," she said eagerly. But instead of replying the fat man wrote something, glanced at her again. "Do I remember this bright little face?" he said softly. " Is it known to me of yore?" At that moment the band began playing; the fat man disappeared. He was tossed away on a great wave of music that came flying over the gleaming floor, breaking the groups up into couples, scattering them, sending them spinning. . . .

Leila had learned to dance at boarding school. Every Saturday afternoon the boarders were hurried off to a little corrugated iron mission hall where Miss Eccles (of London) held her 'select' classes. But the difference between that dusty-smelling hall – with calico texts on the walls, the poor, terrified little woman in a brown velvet toque with rabbit's ears, thumping the cold piano, Miss Eccles poking the girls' feet with her long white wand – and this, was so tremendous that Leila was sure if her partner didn't come and she had to listen to that marvellous music and to watch the others sliding, gliding over the golden floor, she would die at least, or faint, or lift her arms and fly out of one of those dark windows that showed the stars.

"Ours, I think –" Someone bowed, smiled, and offered her his arm; she hadn't to die after all. Someone's hand pressed her waist, and she floated away like a flower that is tossed into a pool.

"Quite a good floor, isn't it?" drawled a faint voice close to her ear.

"I think it's most beautifully slippery," said Leila.

"Pardon!" The faint voice sounded surprised. Leila said it again. And there was a tiny pause before the voice echoed, "Oh, quite!" and she was swung round again.

He steered so beautifully. There was the great difference between dancing with girls and men, Leila decided. Girls banged into each other and stamped on each other's feet; the girl who was the gentleman always clutched you so.

The azaleas were separate flowers no longer; they were pink and white flags streaming by.

"Were you at the Bells' last week?" the voice came again. It sounded tired. Leila wondered whether she ought to ask him if he would like to stop.

"No, this is my first dance," said she.

Her partner gave a little gasping laugh. "Oh, I say," he protested.

"Yes, it is really the first dance I've ever been to." Leila was most fervent. It was such a relief to be able to tell somebody. "You see, I've lived in the country all my life up till now ..."

At that moment the music stopped and they went to sit on two chairs against the wall. Leila tucked her pink satin feet under and fanned herself, while she blissfully watched the other couples passing and disappearing through the swing doors.

"Enjoying yourself, Leila?" asked Jose, nodding her golden head.

Laura passed and gave her the faintest little wink; it made Leila wonder for a moment whether she was quite grown up after all. Certainly her partner did not say very much. He coughed, tucked his handkerchief away, pulled down his waistcoat, took a minute thread off his sleeve. But it didn't matter. Almost immediately the band started and her second partner seemed to spring from the ceiling.

"Floor's not bad," said the new voice. Did one always begin with the floor? And then, "Were you at the Neaves' on Tuesday?" And again Leila explained. Perhaps it was a little strange that her partners were not more interested. For it was thrilling. Her first ball! She was only at the beginning of everything. It seemed to her that she had never known what the night was like before. Up till now it had been dark, silent, beautiful very often – oh yes – but mournful somehow. Solemn. And now it would never be like that again – it had opened dazzling bright.

"Care for an ice?" said her partner. And they went through the swing doors, down the passage, to the supper-room. Her cheeks burned, she was fearfully thirsty. How sweet the ices looked on little glass plates and how cold the frosted spoon was, iced too! And when they came back to the hall there was the fat man waiting for her by the door. It gave her quite a shock again to see how old he was; he ought to have been on the stage with the fathers and mothers. And when Leila compared him with her other partners he looked shabby. His waistcoat was creased, there was a button off his glove, his coat looked as if it was dusty with French chalk.

"Come along, little lady," said the fat man. He scarcely troubled to clasp her, and they moved away so gently, it was more like walking than dancing. But he said not a word about the floor. "Your first dance, isn't it?" he murmured.

"How *did* you know?"

"Ah," said the fat man, "that's what it is to be old!" He wheezed faintly as he steered her past an awkward couple. "You see, I've been doing this kind of thing for the last thirty years."

"Thirty years?" cried Leila. Twelve years before she was born!

"It hardly bears thinking about, does it?" said the fat man gloomily. Leila looked at his bald head, and she felt quite sorry for him.

"I think it's marvellous to be still going on," she said kindly.

"Kind little lady," said the fat man, and he pressed her a little closer and hummed a bar of the waltz. "Of course," he said, "you can't hope to last anything like as long as that. No-o," said the fat man, "long before that you'll be sitting up there on the stage, looking on, in your nice black velvet. And these pretty arms will have turned into little short fat ones, and you'll beat time with such a different kind of fan – a black ebony one." The fat man seemed to shudder. "And you'll smile away like the poor old dears up there, and point to your daughter, and tell the elderly lady next to you how some dreadful man tried to kiss her at the club ball. And your heart will ache, ache" – the fat man squeezed her closer still, as if he really was sorry for that poor heart – "because no one wants to kiss you now. And you'll say how unpleasant these polished floors are to walk on, how dangerous they are. Eh, Mademoiselle Twinkletoes?" said the fat man softly.

Leila gave a light little laugh, but she did not feel like laughing. Was it – could it all be true? It sounded terribly true. Was this first ball only the beginning of her last ball, after all? At that the music seemed to change; it sounded sad, sad; it rose upon a great sigh. Oh, how quickly things changed! Why didn't happiness last for ever? For ever wasn't a bit too long.

"I want to stop," she said in a breathless voice. The fat man led her to the door.

"No," she said, "I won't go outside. I won't sit down. I'll just stand here, thank you." She leaned against the wall, tapping with her foot, pulling up her gloves and trying to smile. But deep inside her a little girl threw her pinafore over her head and sobbed. Why had he spoiled it all?

"I say, you know," said the fat man, "you mustn't take me seriously, little lady."

"As if I should!" said Leila, tossing her small dark head and sucking her underlip. . . .

Again the couples paraded. The swing doors opened and shut. Now new music was given out by the bandmaster. But Leila didn't want to dance any more. She wanted to be home, or sitting on the veranda listening to those baby owls. When she looked through the dark windows at the stars they had long beams like wings . . .

But presently a soft, melting, ravishing tune began, and a young man with curly hair bowed before her. She would have to dance, out of politeness, until she could find Meg. Very stiffly she walked into the middle; very haughtily she put her hand on his sleeve. But in one minute, in one turn, her feet glided, glided. The lights, the azaleas, the dresses, the pink faces, the velvet chairs, all became one beautiful flying wheel. And when her next partner bumped her into the fat man and he said, "Par*don*", she smiled at him more radiantly than ever. She didn't even recognize him again.

Biographical Notes

Katherine Mansfield (1888–1923) is New Zealand's most famous writer. She was the third daughter of a wealthy banker. Her talent first showed at the age of nine, when she won a prize for a school composition.

At the age of fifteen she was sent to school in London. Here she contributed stories to the college literary magazine. At the same time she trained as a cellist at the Royal Academy of Music.

After a two years' stay in New Zealand, she returned to London in 1908. She toured with an opera company and accepted unimportant roles in films to augment her father's annual grant of £100. This period was marked by the death of her beloved brother Leslie in World War I and a number of unhappy love affairs. In 1918 she married the critic, John Middleton Murry. Together with another well-known writer, D. H. Lawrence, they founded a literary magazine.

Her first published book was In a German Pension *(1911), a selection of travel impressions. Her best stories are to be found in the collections* Bliss and Other Stories *(1920),* The Garden Party and Other Stories *(1922),* The Dove's Nest and Other Stories *(1923), and* Something Childish and Other Stories *(published in 1924 after her death).*

From the point of view of literary history, Katherine Mansfield's stories mark a movement away from longer plot-oriented stories to a more psychological description of what has been called a "moment of felt life" (Henry James). She developed new techniques to show the more intimate feelings of her characters.

She died at the age of thirty-five in Fontainebleau, France, where she had gone for medical treatment after suffering from tuberculosis for several years.

Annotations

74 2 **cab** horse-drawn carriage for hire (*modern meaning:* taxi) – 4 **bolster** ['bəʊlstə] kind of cushion – 5 **dress suit** man's formal evening clothes – **to bowl** to move quickly on wheels – 8 **weird** [wɪəd] strange – 10 **fan** instrument used to cool one's face by making the air move – 11 **indifferent** showing no interest or emotion – 13 **Meg** from 'Margaret' – **tuberose** white, sweet-smelling flower (Nachthyazinthe) – **Jose** from 'Josephine' – **loop** *here:* necklace – **amber** yellowish-brown glassy substance used for jewels (Bernstein) – 14 **fur** [fɜ:] jacket or stole made of fur (Pelz) – 15 **pang** sudden feeling of pain – **Laurie** ['lɔ:rɪ] boy's name, short for 'Laurence' – 16 **wisp** small untidy piece of – **tissue paper** thin soft paper used for packing things – 17 **keepsake** souvenir – 19 **Twig?** *sl.* Understand? – 25 **drill hall** gymnasium (Turnhalle) – 27 **gay** happy, cheerful – 31 **to make a dash** to rush, to run quickly – **32 velvet** soft, thick cloth usually made of silk (Samt) – **cloak** loose, sleeveless outer garment (Umhang)

75 2 **to deafen** ['defən] to make deaf, i.e. unable to hear – 3 **to stack** to pile up – **wrap** outer garment, cloak – 4 **apron** ['eɪprən] s.th. worn over one's clothes to keep them clean – **to toss** to throw carelessly – 7 **to quiver** to tremble a little – **jet** *here:* narrow stream (of gas) – 9 **tuning** *here:* the sound of musicians preparing their instruments